SERIOUSLY RICH

SERIOUSLY RICH

The gripping account of a young man whose ruined life was powerfully and radically transformed by God's amazing grace!

Richard Pidgley

Authentic

19 18 17 16 15 14 13   8 7 6 5 4 3 2

Reprinted 2013

First published 2002 by Authentic Media
This third edition published 2010 by Authentic Media Limited
52 Presley Way, Crownhill, Milton Keynes, MK8 0ES
www.authenticmedia.co.uk

British Library Cataloguing in Publication Data

A catalogue record for this book is available from the
British Library

ISBN 978-1-86024-807-8

Cover design by Mark Baker (www.inspiredmedia-uk.com)
Printed and bound by CPI Group (UK) Ltd., Croydon, CR0 4YY

To Lynne, Josh and Sam

Thanks for helping me to follow the call of God on my life. You have given me continuous support and made many sacrifices over the years so I can live the dream. You're amazing and I love you.

CONTENTS

ACKNOWLEDGEMENTS

I would like to thank all my friends who have encouraged me and supported the revision of this book. I would like to particularly thank LMI (Logos Ministries International) who have used this book to help and inspire thousands of young people to explore the Christian faith. Also special thanks to a very dear friend, the late Pat Collyer, who loved God, lived for Jesus and encouraged me to share the Gospel of Jesus Christ with as many people as possible.

This book is a true account of my life, however some names have been changed and place names omitted to protect the privacy of those whom I have mentioned in the book.

FOREWORD

'You are familiar with the generosity of our Master, Jesus Christ. Rich as he was, he gave it all away for us – in one stroke he became poor and we became rich.' [1]

The grace of God is stunning. God's grace links us with his plans that began before time was created and extend beyond the end of time. God's grace lifts us from the depths of human despair to the delights of a relationship with the Father. God's grace liberates us from slavery to the deception and ugliness of sin into the freedom and beauty of his love. And God's grace makes us rich – seriously rich!

God's grace is not found in theological textbooks but in human hearts. God's grace is not a philosophical conclusion made by some irrelevant ecclesiastical council: it is the power of God that transforms hearts and lives. God's grace turns sinners into saints, rebels into royalty and miscreants into ministers. Sin always brings poverty to the human heart, but grace brings God's riches that makes a person rich – seriously rich!

God's grace is personal, lavished upon the world, yet equally applied to individual lives. The story of Richard Pidgley demonstrates the power of God's grace that can reach the individual. What the grace of God has done in Richard's life demonstrates to us all that no need is too great, no place too far, no pit too deep and no moment too late for the grace of God.

Richard Pidgley is a fellow minister of the Gospel. He is a good friend and a brother. And he is seriously rich!

Jeremy Griffiths
Founder and President
The Shepherd's Storehouse International

INTRODUCTION

I was born on the 5 February 1966 in Poole, Dorset. I didn't come into the world on my own, because not long after I was born, Colin my twin brother also arrived. My family was plagued by many problems such as crime, gambling and drink. As a toddler I was not aware of the full extent of my parents' petty criminal empire, but as I grew older more was revealed to me. According to my mum, my real dad disputed his fatherhood of Colin and me. He blamed our arrival on somebody such as the milkman! So, with this major difficulty in the marriage, my parents decided to break up: I was 18 months old. This resulted in Colin and me being placed in various foster homes, sometimes together and sometimes apart.

This book is a true account of my life, one that started in a broken home and led to a dank prison cell. I have been honest in recalling my life as it happened. I have no wish to glorify my past, but have written in such a way that you, the reader, can comprehend the wonderful change that has taken place since Jesus Christ came into my heart. This book relates how I discovered true treasure in Jesus Christ: a treasure that turned my ruined life of shame and waste into wealth, literally overnight!

This is a story that will inspire genuine hope for all those from broken homes, hope for those held prisoners to sin, hope for those desperately looking for love and acceptance, hope for parents worried about their children who are on drugs and into crime. As the words of the songwriter said . . .

> It is no secret what God can do.
> What he's done for others, he'll do for you.[2]

The Bible declares: *'Those who become Christians become new persons. They are not the same anymore, for the old life is gone. A new life has begun!'*[3]

1

EARLY DAYS

Terry and Sally Smith were a couple in their forties, who had never been able to have children of their own. Because of their love for children they became foster parents, and in this they excelled. Thinking back over the years, I can remember them telling us of many other children who they had counted it a privilege to foster. They had had children from deprived areas of London for summer holidays by the seaside and also longer-term placements.

Terry was a carpenter, and a very good one at that. He had a large garage by the side of the house filled with tools and was always doing little jobs for people. He worked for a company by Poole Quay and was the yard foreman. My fond memories of him were of a man who was gentle and peace loving. I never heard him quarrel with people, but felt his hurt as he became upset when others fought and fell out. He was a great lover of going along steadily, 'keeping his nose clean' as he put it. He was strict when he needed to be and I can remember going over his knees on more than one occasion for a spanking, which I am sure I rightly deserved! Terry didn't have any hobbies as such, for most of his spare time was spent looking after his aged mum and two aunts. He would chop firewood for them and mow their lawns. Almost every Saturday night we would all go with him to visit the family. After doing all the chores, with which I would help him, Terry would sit down in a well-worn armchair and listen to the family news from the lips of his mum or aunts. They loved to look after him as well, making him supper of ham sandwiches and home-made bread pudding that he enjoyed so much.

Sally was a mum to me – I went to her screaming with my first bee sting! I went to her with sticky fingers to wipe, and she would sit by my bed many a night waiting for me to drop off to sleep. She just loved children: black, white or yellow it didn't matter. She would spend hours with all sorts of kids. We must have worn her out – she wasn't getting any younger – as we wanted to do this and that. But she took it all in her stride, and I know now that we aged both her and Terry. She never moaned about her rights as an individual in the home, making sacrifices all the time so the rest of us had what we needed. I am glad though now – years on from the nightmare of my youth – that I can still pick up the phone and call her 'Mum'.

Both Terry and Sally Smith gave us love and welcomed us into their home. They did what they could to help two little boys find the love and acceptance that all children need. As we grew, so did the pressures on that little home, pressure that Terry and Sally's health finally couldn't cope with. I want to honour them, along with all foster parents who give their lives selflessly to children, doing all that they possibly can.

> *I want to honour them along with all foster parents who give their lives selflessly to children*

Often they are hurt and abused by the system. Often they are financially worse off. Tired physically and mentally, but loving children all the same, they do it all just to see the smiles upon their little faces.

Colin and I were very young when we were placed with the Smiths: so young I can't remember accurately much before that time. One of my earliest memories at the Smiths' was being pushed in a pushchair beside a duck pond. I was allowed out of the buggy and toddled by the waterside held securely by a rein, which was leather with a little blue breastplate. The sun was shining, the memories of whatever had happened before were clouded, and for now I was happy, secure in the love that Terry and Sally Smith were giving me.

I can remember being bathed in the kitchen sink! I guess I was pretty small then, as I sat in that sink playing with a cup and splashing around in what seemed to be gallons of water. I remember that, along with millions of other kids, I hated the soap getting in my eyes. Mrs Smith would be as careful as she could, but paranoia would set in and screams would be heard! I laugh now as I bathe Sam, my youngest son, and hear him squeal as he too hates the soap getting near his face.

I can remember being bathed in the kitchen sink

The Smiths loved us and for a while everything looked as if it would work out wonderfully. We had settled in well and so, after a few years, the Smiths wanted to make the arrangement more secure and permanent for them and also for Colin and me. They applied to adopt us, and so the wheels began to move as social workers and other professionals made their assessments. The whole thing would have been a 'happy ever after' story except for one thing. That one thing proved

The whole thing would have been a 'happy ever after' story except for one thing

to be an obstacle that nobody was going to be able to remove. My real mother!

She had been allowed access to Colin and me every now and again. In fact, I didn't think of her as my mum at all. We would be taken to a social services office in Lower Parkstone. Once, after trust had been built, the social worker would allow her to walk Colin and me in the small park. I can remember all her questions about Terry and Sally Smith and whether we were happy there or not. She would bring different presents for us on those trips in a bid to buy affection, but no matter how many gifts she brought, which I later found out were stolen, I could not bring myself to like her. I would feel uncomfortable and would recoil from her as she went to kiss and hug me at the end of the visits. Years later when I questioned her about this time in my life, she told me that although she knew both Colin and I were happy at the Smiths and that it would have been the best for us, she couldn't let go of us. She said she resented the Smiths having us and was jealous of them. When the final decision on adoption was made, the answer was no, because of my mother's unwillingness to let us go – although she would not have been able to have us herself at the time.

That was a blow to Terry and Sally, as they had done such a good job with two little boys. We were part of their family and treated as such by all their relatives. The Smiths wanted the security of adoption, as they didn't want the hurt of having us, who they regarded as their sons, torn from them.

Their desire to have their own child legally led them to approach the social services regarding the possibility of having another child. The day came when two suddenly became three! Natalie, a beautiful girl, just two years old, came into the home one day and Colin and I found ourselves with a sister. Things seemed to work out well, as we took to Natalie and played with her for hours, just as any other young family would do. But unbeknown to me, storm clouds were gathering on the horizon all the time.

Springdale Infant School

The day the playgroup took us to see Springdale Infant School was a challenge to my security. It's not fair; as soon as you get used to something like the familiar sights and sounds of a playgroup, they whisk you off to a very different and even threatening place. I had grown to enjoy playgroup and liked all the teachers. I was confident in the surrounds of the United Reformed Church hall and would often don a large tall hat and cape and go around kissing all the ladies, much to everyone's amusement! Nothing stays the same for long though, and before I knew it, a teacher had come from the infant school to read us all a story and also to introduce herself. The next week came round and we found ourselves on a guided tour of the school, being shown all the classrooms and playgrounds that we would be using the very next term.

Once I had settled into school my confidence rose, and before long I had made new friends with children who had come from other Broadstone playgroups. In fact, I rapidly became a gang leader, which wasn't bad for a kid of my age. My gang was highly feared by the other children because we had this great game called 'Charge of the light brigade'. I would gather my mounted lancers at one end of the playing field and we would put the fine dusty dirt into the pockets of our shorts. Then, at my command of 'Charge', we would run from one side of the field to the other, leaping over and running through any group of children playing in our way. We would also sprinkle the dirt from our pockets as we charged, to give the authentic dust cloud coming from the horses' hooves. This game I had invented was fun for my gang, but not much fun for anyone in our way! The dinner ladies tried to

My gang was highly feared by the other children

stop us charging around, but rebellion was setting in and I took no notice of their constant appeals to calm down or threats of having to sit inside during playtimes.

Thief

On the whole, I wasn't too badly behaved – or so I thought! But the day soon came when I was publicly branded a thief before the whole school. I had gone into the school office one lunchtime to see a teacher and discovered that no one was there. I spotted a first aid box open on the office desk. Looking inside, I saw a tube with a lid on that looked pretty interesting: so interesting in fact that I whipped it out of the box and stuffed it in my shorts' pocket. Out in the school playing field, I found a quiet corner and proceeded to examine my 'booty'. Inside the tube was a glass thing that I later learned was a rather expensive thermometer. Curious about the 'red stuff' inside, I smashed the glass vial only to see the red liquid quickly soak into the hot dry ground of the field. I suddenly heard the school bell signifying the end of lunch break. Shoving the plastic tube down the front of my shorts this time, I ran to the yard and lined up with my class waiting to be led into the building by a teacher.

Suddenly my heart stopped. Could I be hearing correctly? They were calling my name out and telling me to come to the front of the school parade. Standing in front of all the other kids, the deputy head, a male teacher, lifted up my shirt and pulled out the plastic tube that had protected the thermometer and held it high for all to see. I was now shamed, and I knew I had done something very wrong. I was then escorted by the deputy head to the headmistress' office and questioned about my crime. To make matters worse, Mrs Smith was called up to the school and, after I had promised to pay back the cost of a new thermometer out of my pocket money, I was taken home early that day in disgrace.

Although I was settled at the Smiths', I was confused when letters were sent from the school to home. Often in the classroom they would read out the surnames of the parents and the appropriate child would cry out 'yes' and raise their hand up to receive the envelope to take home. When they read out 'Mr and Mrs Smith' I had to respond, but because they were called Smith and my name was Pidgley, I felt very uncomfortable and wondered what everyone else was thinking. I hated those times, squirming in my chair feeling hot and bothered, faced flushed as the teacher began calling out surnames beginning with 'S'. Although things were happy at the Smiths' home, deep inside my heart the feelings of anxiety and questions like 'Who am I?' rose to the surface. They threatened my little world and made me insecure and often robbed me of many hours of sleep. I remember to this day Mrs Smith sitting by my bedside for hours trying to get me to go to sleep. She knew I was troubled, but all her loving coaxing could not bring me to vocalise my deepest fears.

2

GROWING PAINS

Bandit

The 'egg farm' was about two miles or so away from where we lived. It was a type of farm shop that was little more than a tottering wooden shack at the end of a dusty lane. The outside didn't promise much, but, on entering the shed, a small child was faced with all the delights of Aladdin's cave! For there were shelves of sweets, Mojos, Blackjacks, Fruit Salads, Sherbet Fountains and then those unattainable chocolate delights that our pocket money could never stretch to – the Cadbury range – wow! Every time I went to the egg farm my eyes would almost pop out of their sockets and, because of my waywardness, the chocolate bars were soon stuffed in my pockets!

Now I knew that stealing was absolutely wrong and I also knew what it was to have a great big guilty conscience, but that was something I thought I could handle. The days we went to the egg farm were days of high adventure. We rode our bikes along the roads leading to the outskirts of Broadstone, where the farm was situated. We laughed and had such glee on our faces as we declared to each other that we were bandits! Once at the farm it was easy – too easy. One of us would keep look-out while the rest of us stuffed our pockets with sweets. Sometimes we were very bold and actually paid for about two pennies worth of Mojos, while we carried away almost all the egg farm stock from the shelves in our pockets.

We never got caught. Maybe the owners suspected us, but they never challenged us about the disappearance of so much stock during those long hot days of the summer holiday. The egg farm experience bolstered my confidence as a sneak thief, looking out for opportunities to make a killing.

Of course stealing was wrong! I knew that, but if other people had plenty, did it really matter? Andrew, a school-mate, had everything! Well it seemed that way as I gazed around his bedroom. At that time of my life Action Man was the 'in toy'; every schoolboy had an Action Man and the lucky ones had all the best outfits and the accessories. Andrew's bedroom looked like a showroom for Palitoy, the maker of the plastic hero. You name it, from deep-sea diver to space man, Andrew had all the Action Man uniforms. I, on the other hand, didn't have many and so the only way to get more Action Man uniforms seemed to be by stealing them from Andrew.

Andrew was very trusting, and before long we were best of mates, or so he thought. I would ask him if we could play Action Man and when he said, 'Yes,' I would visit him after school. His mum would open the door to me, a young tearaway carrying a naked Action Man, and I would rush into the house. We would play for hours in the bedroom and when Andrew's mum shouted that it was time for me to go home, she never seemed to recognise that my Action Man was leaving with a set of clothes, and often with an arsenal that would put 'Rambo' to shame!

The Little Rec

Beside Springdale Infant School there was a small recreation ground that we called the 'Little Rec'. It had swings, a slide, a seesaw and an excellent witches hat that was constantly being damaged, as the bigger kids would somehow take the hat off its pivot at the top. The witches hat became the rigging of a pirate ship for us! We spent hours rocking back and forth and spinning round on that thing. Thankfully, I never came to any harm, although I knew of some kids who had fallen off and broken their arms.

The Little Rec also had a great dirt track path running from the main road right through the middle of the park, turning up a hill and leading to the council's garage, where all the green-keeping equipment was kept. For my seventh birthday I was given a bike, which I loved, and Colin and I would race the other kids in what we called 'Speedway' down the dirt track. The summer months were the best because as we sped down the dirt track, dust would go flying all over the place, and as we skidded to a halt at the end of the racetrack we would be lost in a cloud. We would also stick a piece of card into the spokes of the wheels so that we had an 'authentic' engine sound as we sped along.

The Little Rec became my domain. I had a gang of kids hanging out with me, and most of the time they did what I said. We broke the windows of the council garage, we started small fires, and we'd climb onto the roof of the Wendy house and make a general nuisance of ourselves. Bit by bit, this would filter back to Mr and Mrs Smith. They were very good and although they told me off when it was needed, they also loved me in their correction.

The Little Rec was as I said, a 'paradise' for a little gang leader such as myself; I got up to all sorts of mischief. One summer's day as the holidays became boring, I climbed a tall tree in the park, then Colin and two others from my gang went and telephoned the fire station using the 999 number. Wow, it was something to see a beautiful big red fire engine approach the park! The lights were flashing and the siren blaring as it came to a stop right under my tree. I could have easily got down, but I had to be rescued now and this delighted the gang members as a burly fire-man gently helped their leader down the ladder. They took my details and sure enough Mrs Smith asked me about it later that day. I was told not to climb the trees again and never to waste the fire service's time with such pranks. Being told that they could have been rescuing somebody in a real fire rather than wasting their time on us did not, however, sink into my heart at that time. To me it was just a good laugh and, after all, I didn't care about anybody else anyway.

At the very top of the park was a little stream that ran alongside the school playing field and eventually went under a fence into a man's back garden. That stream was too big a temptation to resist. Parts of the stream were not too deep and when I had my wellies on I could wade up the stream being sure to keep to the sides so as not to have wet socks. This was like wading up some South American rain forest stream: the trees were so low over the water I would pretend to cut back the undergrowth and make a path for those following me. Using branches from the willow trees, we would swing like Tarzan over the water. Often there

There would be a cracking noise and a splash as a branch gave way and someone ended up in the stream

would be a cracking noise and a splash as a branch gave way and someone ended up in the stream. We would shout and howl as this happened.

All the noise of splashing water and screaming boys attracted the attention of the man who lived in the garden into which the stream flowed. He would come out of his garden through a little gate and bellow at us, reminding us constantly that it was private land and that we were trespassing. I forget his name, but remember that he looked a little like Edward Heath, and seeing his red face explode made it all the more fun. In fact, we would go on raiding parties right up to his garden and poke our heads under the fence where the stream flowed. Sometimes, if we were particularly bold, we would shout obscenities at him as he sat lounging in the sun on his patio. Sometimes, when we encouraged each other to go a step further in devilment, we would throw dirt bombs that would explode all over his immaculate lawns and crash into his prized flower beds. He would run after us, but luckily he was too old and overweight to catch us.

The man complained to Mrs Smith on several occasions, but when I was asked about upsetting the 'nice' man with the beautiful garden living next to the school, I blatantly denied it.

Lying was becoming a habit of mine, which I thought I had mastered quite well. I noticed at home that if I did something wrong and Colin and I were asked about it, if I kept an innocent face and kept calm, Colin would get all flustered and get the blame! This was most entertaining, as Colin would often get all sorts of punishments that I rightly deserved: the halo around my head would shine so brightly as I lied about things increasingly and watched my brother getting punished.

The Building Site

Every boy loves a building site: there is so much with which to meddle and play. There are all those mounds of dirt with hard sods on top – an ammunition dump for kids who want to play war and like throwing dirt bombs at people; brick and wall ties make good boomerangs or Chinese throwing stars; and walls that have just been laid are fun to push over. There are ladders to climb and scaffolding to run along and from which to lob dirt bombs. The games I could play on a building site were endless. When the signs from the construction company went up on the piece of land next to the school, adjoining the Little Rec, it seemed like heaven to a small, naughty boy!

We were told time and time again to stay away, as the lorries rolled into town carrying bricks, sand and planks, etc. Building sites are dangerous, they told us – and so they are – but this one was too big a temptation to resist.

We played war for hours: it was great fun throwing dirt bombs at people! If the bomb missed somebody and hit a brick wall, the sand and cement would explode on impact into a cloud of dust, thus making it look a realistic bomb to a small boy. However, if it hit its target, it didn't always explode! An unexploded bomb always hurt, but I didn't care – after all, war had its casualties!

The builders must have got fed up with all the damage we did night after night. After our tea, we would lie in wait for the men to knock off and then we would strike. We'd take our positions in our imaginary trenches and behind the shelled ruins and then, when we were ready, I would yell at the top of my voice, 'War!' and the bombing would start. To this day I am surprised that none of us ever got seriously hurt as we threw stones, half bricks, in fact anything that came to hand, at one another.

All good things come to an end, or so they say, and our war games on the building site came to an abrupt end one Friday night. We had already had a week of war games, causing much havoc for the builders as they came in each morning. We waited over in the Little Rec and as the builders cleared off for the weekend we closed in like a band of commandos ready to take our positions as before. This time, however, it all went horribly wrong, terribly wrong, for as we slipped into the half-built houses and began to climb the scaffolding, we were suddenly ambushed by a gang of builders who had been hiding.

Their counter-attack worked well, as we were all caught instantaneously and rounded up together as prisoners of war

The roughneck builders must have got so fed up with the vandalism that they had a war strategy of their own! Their counter-attack worked well, as we were all caught instantaneously and rounded up together as prisoners of war.

Unfortunately for me, they soon realised that I was the commander of the small, defeated band. After a few questions were answered, six of the other boys, along with myself, were flung into the back of the pick-up lorry that had doubled back to fool us. Under guard, we were all marched down the drive of the Smiths' home in great humiliation and shame. The builders didn't mince their words as they brought the charges of damage and havoc caused by our war games, which must have been very embarrassing to Mr and Mrs Smith. They pacified the builders, who were threatening to call the police, by promising to tell us off and to make sure we wouldn't be playing war again on the building site. The builders left, and not long afterwards, so did my mates, leaving me to face the music!

Fire

I remember that during the winter Mrs Smith would make a real fire using chopped wood and coal in the lounge fire grate. Mr Smith would chop up the firewood skilfully with an axe, and I would stand for hours bagging the wood with him on cold Saturday afternoons. He never said much at those times, apart from the fact that he considered it his duty to look after his aunties at Wimborne and his mother, who lived at Blandford, by providing firewood for them.

Whenever Mrs Smith built a fire in the lounge grate, I would ask to light it and she would allow me to do the honours. She would tell me that I was allowed to do this, firstly, because she was supervising me and secondly, because she hoped that I would never go anywhere and start fires on my own. She meant well, but an unhealthy interest in fire-making had already been ignited deep within me and no amount of warnings about the danger of matches would deter me in my quest to explore the way of fire.

One day, when everyone was out of the house, I discovered where the matches were hidden. I would often poke my face into cupboards and drawers once the coast was clear. In the kitchen there was a tall larder cupboard above the fridge, with lots of shelves filled with Tupperware and cake tins, etc. This cupboard was out of bounds, but there comes a time when all children ask the question 'why?' Having asked myself that question, and knowing the coast was clear, I decided to investigate the forbidden place. Among things that were not that interesting to a boy – unless he is into cake making – I found, on the second shelf, a plain cardboard packet with about five brand new matchboxes inside it.

Now, this was a big discovery for a boy like me. Once I knew where the matches were kept the sky was the limit for my experimentation with fire.

I had watched Mr Smith in his garden shed take a strong-smelling purple liquid from a large metal container with a little tap fixed at the bottom. He called this purple liquid 'paraffin', and I noticed that he would put some of it in a heater in his large, cold garage and it burned. I also noted that things marked 'flammable' burned well. I had gained an understanding, without letting on or giving any cause for suspicion, and I knew that if I waited, the time would come when I could have lots of fun. I knew that it was wrong; I also knew that it was highly dangerous, but there was a compelling desire to do my own thing.

I would often wait until Mrs Smith went out or was busy in the house and also until Colin was out of the way. I didn't trust him and knew that, under pressure, he would crack and tell the truth, and that would never do. I must have drained that massive barrel of paraffin over the next few weeks. I loved going into that musty old shed and stealing away with a tissue soaked in paraffin, ready to ignite behind the shed at the bottom of the garden. It was amazing that I never set the shed alight with my experiments. A stray match in the store shed would have sent the roof flying, as the paraffin barrel would have exploded along with all the other bottles marked 'flammable'.

Andrew was fascinated by the tales of my paraffin experiments and asked me to take some matches up to his house. I had managed to steal a whole box of matches, which was very risky, as Mrs Smith was still in the house. I got on my bike and cycled all the way up the road as fast as I could to Andrew's house. Alongside Andrew's house was a plot of land that had once had a home upon it. The house was long gone, but the foundations and the cellar remained and were filled with stagnant water. This was another magnet, drawing boys like me to its unfathomable depths.

Andrew and I quickly went onto the 'jungle' plot and found some tall grass growing up the fence of an adjoining house and garden shed. All it took was just one match. I can remember the fear and exhilaration as Andrew and I ran from the inferno that threatened to burn the shed down and spread to the house. We crouched down in the undergrowth, hidden from the frantic house owners and neighbours who had sprung into action in a bid to extinguish the fierce flames. As they began to empty the pool of stagnant water with buckets, which they repeatedly carried to the scene of the fire, we could hear the sirens of the fire engines getting louder and louder as the appliances sped up the road. It was a good job we were hiding – to be seen at this time would have incriminated us as the arsonists.

We could hear the sirens of the fire engines getting louder and louder as the appliances sped up the road

I knew, once again, I had done a silly and very dangerous thing. The possibility of people burning to death didn't really cross my mind, but the buzz of starting a fire sure felt good, and was something that I would repeat many times in the years to follow.

Smoking

Mr Smith used to smoke and had done so since he was a young man. His Aunt Mary, who lived at Wimborne, would also light up a cigarette in front of young eyes. I would watch as grown-ups lit up and inhaled that delicious-looking smoke. I would hold my breath as the smoke disappeared from view. Where it went I didn't know, but it always came out again, and that was a trick that I really wanted to learn. Once, when Mr Smith became ill and was off work, he decided to quit the habit. Whether for financial reasons or health reasons I can't remember, but I do remember him constantly chewing gum or sucking mints afterwards. Because Mr Smith had quit smoking I was not going to have a chance to experiment with his tobacco, and so I had to bide my time.

My big break came when I was nearly nine years old. A couple of mates and I had gone into Broadstone on our bikes, and as I rode along I noticed that it was bin day and people had put their bins out. As I came near to the end of the road, a man came out of his gate, saw the bins, put his bag down and went back into his garden to fetch his bin. I quickly stopped by the man's open bag, which had been left on the pavement, and there, for all to see, was a brand new packet of cigarettes. I couldn't help myself (as I later discovered a good opportunist thief is always on the look-out for something to steal). Like a bird of prey swooping for the kill, my little hand dived into the bag and seized those cigarettes for myself. Heart beating wildly, I was off on my bike once more and around the corner before the man reappeared with his bin! Now I was going to have some great fun.

I rode to the Little Rec with my two friends and we hid the packet of cigarettes under a brick, alongside the wall of the council garage. Cycling home, I knew we were on a mission. I had to get hold of some matches – for cigarettes without matches would be no fun at all. We all had a drink of squash and then went out into the garden. I doubled back into the house and again, at great risk of being caught red-handed by Mrs Smith, set out to get matches from the tall larder cupboard in the kitchen. Once again, I was lucky and wasn't caught. With the matches shoved down the front of my trousers, I went and found Mrs Smith busy cleaning in the bedrooms. On gaining permission to go back to the Little Rec, we went flying off once more. Lying down in the long grass we each held a cigarette. How big we all thought we looked, how grown up and sophisticated we felt, as we lit up and inhaled the first lungful of deadly smoke. Those first cigarettes were a novelty – in fact, we got through the whole packet of twenty in one afternoon!

Little did I suspect the awful addiction those cigarettes would bring upon me – years of slavery to the cruel taskmaster called Nicotine. It was the start of an addiction that would have me at its mercy for many years and lower me to such depths of indignity as I craved for my nicotine fix. When I had no money for cigarettes, I would make cigars from leaves in the woods. I would use dry blackberry and bramble leaves, crushed and rolled up in public toilet paper, in a bid to feed my smoking habit.

Later, when I was at school, I would steal cigarettes from one of the teachers and have a quick puff in the toilets by the gym. The secret was to steal just one cigarette each night, that way she never caught on that she was feeding my illicit addiction.

I thought I was incredibly grown up when, at the age of 15, I bought myself a pipe! What a sight as people walked past a bench in Poole Park and watched me puffing on a pipe, as if I was some old man sitting in the sun, soaking up the warm rays and fondly remembering some past event.

There was a shop on the corner of a parade of shops near the park that sold papers, sweets and cigarettes of all sorts.

The owner was an older man who was unscrupulous in his business transactions with young kids. Even if you couldn't see over his counter, if you had the money you could have any type of tobacco that you liked. I loved nothing more than buying a nice cigar on a summer's day and then going into the park. Then, when I was seated on a branch of my favourite tree, I would light up, enjoying the mellow flavour and aromatic smell as I smoked my cigar, and watched the day pass by.

I can remember people warning us that if we smoked we would be hooked and also that we could die of lung cancer. However, when you're young and not even a teenager, when you're someone who thinks you have your whole life yet to live, lung cancer is not a consideration. If you get hooked, so what! It's what you enjoy doing, isn't it? And so it was that I became hooked on nicotine. The craving for a cigarette didn't happen overnight, but it did come. So anyone who thinks they can try it and control it, be warned. Thousands today are desperately trying to quit and, through the effort of trying to be free from nicotine, they are now realising the full strength of addiction and its mighty hold on their lives. I pity anyone now who is trying to break free from the power of smoking. I know firsthand the awful feeling of dependence for that cigarette as you wake up. That instinctive reaching for the cigarette as you finish your meal. The anxious feeling if you run out late at night and you know the shops will be shut. My addiction was awful, and only the power of God could set me free.

> *My addiction was awful, and only the power of God could set me free*

As I remember those early days at Broadstone, I think
of happy times: times of fun and laughter, when the sun
seemed to shine all the time. However, clouds were on the
horizon that would blot out the sun, leaving me in the
cold shade – a darkness that would block out the warmth
and light for years to come.

3

BOARDING SCHOOL

One beautiful summer's day, our Persian social worker came to visit us. She brought with her, as an offering to gain our friendship, some used postage stamps from Persia. She then took Colin and me for a walk, individually, in the back garden for a chat. She began to explain to me that Mr and Mrs Smith had not been feeling so well of late; also, that they were extremely tired and that it would help them if we changed school. She then asked me if I would like to go for a drive with her, Mrs Smith and Colin into the New Forest to see a new school that we could go to if we liked.

I wonder now just how much choice we had, if any. Knowing the social services of the time, I guess we really had no choice! But she was good at her job, and she soon told us all the good things about the school as we sped along the dual carriageway.

The school was a preparatory boarding school for the very young up to secondary education age. It had originally been a girls' school, but had relocated some years before to this amazing manor house. The old house was rich in history, having served as a hideout for Loyalists to the Crown during the English Civil War. The owner had bravely hidden soldiers fleeing from Oliver Cromwell's men and had paid for it with her life, being caught, tried and sentenced to death. Because of the house's bloody history, it was reputed to have been haunted by those executed by the Roundheads under Oliver Cromwell. I never saw any apparitions of the ghostly kind, but on many occasions I had fearful nightmares and felt an icy cold, evil, almost suffocating presence in the small hours as I ventured to use the bathroom. There was a secret closet there, in which the Cavaliers had hidden before being caught by the Roundheads.

> *I had fearful nightmares and felt an icy cold, evil, almost suffocating presence*

The house had three floors. On the ground floor were reception rooms, staff rooms, classrooms and common rooms. The other two floors were filled with dormitories and bathrooms. The grounds were extensive, covering acres, with paddocks and beautiful rhododendrons bushing out along the borders of what seemed like a jungle to small children. There were the remains of a Second World War air raid shelter that we played in for hours and hours. The roof had long gone, but we ran along the top of the walls, leaping across the gaps and narrowly avoiding injury as we barely made it. Then there was the plantation adjoining the school grounds, and, if you climbed through the hole in the fence, you could walk for what seemed miles.

The school had bike sheds and an outside swimming pool, which I broke one year by throwing a sharp stone onto the ice on a frosty day. The stone bounced along the ice ripping into the vinyl liner along the side wall. When the ice melted my sin was fully revealed and I had the slipper from the headmaster.

When we rolled up the front drive of the school that
first afternoon, the taste of adventure and something new
had a great appeal. The headmaster seemed strict, but
said all the right things to lure two boys into saying 'Yes'
to his school. We were given a guided tour around the
school – all the best bits of course! We were shown a dormitory with only three beds in it, and a bathroom with
one bath, which we later learned was for staff only.

Later that day, as our social worker drove us home,
she asked what we thought of the school. Both Colin and
I chirped up from the back of the car that it looked great.
Then she asked us whether, if she could arrange it, which
would probably take some doing, we would like to go
there? When we said yes, we didn't realise that it would
be the start of a new chapter in our lives. In fact, our life
with the Smiths was coming to a close, and Colin and I
would not be together for much longer. If I had known
then the pain I was about to go through in the next few
months, I would have never agreed to go. Upon reflection,
I now realise that it would have been impossible for Colin
or me to stay with Terry and Sally Smith, for our behaviour had become so bad that it was the final nail in the
coffin.

The summer holidays came and went very quickly that
year. There was much excitement as our new school uniforms were bought and Mrs Smith sewed our names onto
everything, socks and all.

The September term began and I realised that with it I
had started a whole new life. Once Mr and Mrs Smith had
gone, Colin and I were taken upstairs to our dormitory,
and we then realised that the room we were now placed
in was not the one we had seen earlier on our first visit!
This dormitory had eight beds in it and we were suddenly exposed to public school life.

Miss Collins the matron – or 'Colley', as everyone, staff and children alike, affectionately knew her – began to go through our possessions. She went through everything, like a trained customs officer, with nothing escaping her beady eye. My penknife was taken instantly, much to my displeasure. At the interview the headmaster had assured me that I could have my penknife with me – after all, this had been a deciding factor for me in going to the school in the first place! Colley had a heart of gold; and she always wore a spotlessly clean white coat. She had a red face and a mop of white hair to match the brilliance of her coat. She was strict and took no prisoners, but had a way about her that won the children's hearts.

She went through everything, like a trained customs officer

Discipline can be unpleasant for anyone: after all, we all want to do our own thing. Yet with discipline there is a great degree of security, and security brings peace. Small children away from home need peace, especially for those first few days. Colley introduced us to the other six boys sharing the dormitory. They were all old hands, at seven to nine years of age, and they looked at us with suspicion, probably wondering how long we would last the new regime! We were marched down to the dining room for supper – a glass of milk and some cake – then swiftly marched back up to the bathroom, where we lined up to use the loos and to brush our teeth.

Once we were in bed, Colley read out the riot act. Potential offenders were warned of the dreaded 'Colley's jobs' that took place on Saturday mornings for anyone who stepped over the line. Those jobs were feared and hated by all the children: cleaning, dusting, mopping and polishing, etc, while all the other children were having free time and playing elsewhere around the school grounds.

As soon as the lights went off the interrogation started. 'What's your name?' 'Where do you come from?' 'What does your dad do?' I began to answer the questions, hoping to give an acceptable reply, when suddenly the door flung open and the door frame was filled with the awesome sight of Colley! I said she was strict, so, first night or not, we all ended up doing Colley's jobs that first Saturday morning!

The first term went very quickly. We didn't get a chance to feel homesick because so much was happening all the time. Every day I was making new friends, literally from the four corners of the earth. There were children whose parents were government officials and the like, from China, Africa and even Papua New Guinea.

Sadness

I had settled down well at school and enjoyed the routine of public school life. However, like all the children, I looked forward to going home for the holidays, sleeping in my own bed, having all my toys around me, playing in my old stomping grounds, and being loved and cuddled by Mr and Mrs Smith. The autumn term had flown by and now we were going home for the Christmas holiday.

Like all children, I loved the excitement of Christmas, and I wrote out the list to Father Christmas of toys I wanted, unaware that another big change was going to occur in my life. Those few days before Christmas had an air of menace about them. Mr and Mrs Smith seemed tense, and I had an uneasy feeling that all was not well, yet I could not put my finger upon what. Christmas Day came, and as usual we leapt out of bed and ripped open the packages that Father Christmas had left the night before. After lunch, Mrs Smith took me to one side and she had tears welling up in her eyes as she told me that Colin and I would be going to see our real mother on Boxing Day.

I had never felt comfortable with my real mum or with her common-law husband. In fact there was something sinister about him that gave me the creeps. I remember protesting that I didn't want to go, but Mrs Smith explained that we had to, even though she didn't seem happy about it herself.

That Boxing Day was the worst day of my young life. It was the day I felt that my heart had been torn out and I wanted to die. We had breakfast, and afterwards I was surprised to see Mr Smith putting many of our belongings, such as toys and bags of our clothes, into the car. Why did we need so much for one day? The journey was quiet. By now the tension was getting unbearable, and when we pulled up outside my real mum's house both Mr and Mrs Smith had eyes that were filling with tears. They knocked on the door and, although my mum greeted us with a big smile, I felt an awful sense of foreboding: something was dreadfully wrong. I felt nervous, like an animal lining up outside the slaughterhouse, knowing and sensing something is wrong, but being unable to do anything about it.

> *That Boxing Day was the worst day of my young life. It was the day I felt that my heart had been torn out and I wanted to die*

The Smiths kissed us and hugged us and then they were suddenly gone. If I had known then what I would discover hours later, I wouldn't have let go of them. In fact, I would have refused to even enter the house. Mum tried to make an effort and her 'husband' smiled at us, but through his smile I felt unwelcome and a nuisance to him. After a bit of lunch, which I didn't feel like eating, and with a lump in my throat, I asked the fateful question: 'When are we going home?' Mum said, 'Didn't the Smiths tell you that you aren't going home?' Everything spun around in my mind. The feeling of foreboding now made sense. Tears began to flow down my face as I said I wanted to go home. Her 'husband' began to get cross with me and shouted at me, accusing me of being ungrateful. I cried all the more and he shouted all the more. They put me in the front room on my own and so I cried all afternoon. I was desperate to go back to the Smiths' house, my home, and yet it was impossible.

That night someone came to baby-sit Colin and me as Mum and her husband were going out drinking. As we lay on put-up beds in the front room, I sobbed and sobbed. Colin was quiet. I don't think he realised the full horror of what had happened to us. I was still crying in the early hours as they came home. I remember the fear deep inside my quivering heart as he began to swear at Mum and hit her because it was all her fault that Colin and I were in his house. He shouted and screamed all sorts of obscenities at Mum, Colin and me. The tears flowed and flowed into the next day. In fact, when morning came, I was in such an emotional state with puffy eyes, that Mum called the social services out as an emergency. Two ladies came to see us about mid-morning. I was so badly affected by the events of the past day that I couldn't even talk to them coherently. It was obvious to these young women that a big mistake had been made and that they were dealing with a young boy who was absolutely broken-hearted. They told me that, for all sorts of reasons, I could not go back to the Smiths, but I wasn't listening to them because of all my sobbing. Colin had also heard the shouting the night before, and his story corroborated mine. Hearing all this made the women social workers concerned for our safety. They had a chat with Mum, and within minutes all our kit was packed again, and this time we were in the car heading for the Bournemouth Observation and Assessment Centre.

As we lay on put-up beds in the front room, I sobbed and sobbed. Colin was quiet. I don't think he realised the full horror of what had happened to us

That place was a nightmare. I thought I had problems! Kids were brought to that place from the types of situation that luridly fill the front pages of the tabloids. The staff were neither loving nor caring. Now, as the extent of abuse in children's homes throughout the seventies is being revealed, I can well believe what the people who went through those homes as children are saying. Thankfully, those days at the O and A Centre were short-lived, as the next school term came round quickly.

Once back at school, I felt, initially, a sense of relief: at least I was in familiar surroundings again and that helped a little. But the sight of the other kids hugging and waving goodbye to their parents until they would meet again, was all too much for me. That night I laid my head down to sleep, but sleep was far from me as my mind was awash with all sorts of disturbing things: Who would love me now? Who would look after me? Where do I go from here? Such thoughts, and the memories of being at Broadstone with the Smiths, churned my tattered emotions and the tears began to flow. I kept as quiet as I could, as a river of salty tears flowed upon my pillow, which was soon saturated. I struggled with my breathing, as anxiety engulfed my mind and I felt wave after wave of panic buffet me like breakers upon the rocks. Yet I dared not make a sound, lest anyone else should know I had been crying. I already had the shame of having no one in the world and no home in the world. I could not add to that the indignity of a nine-year-old boy sobbing – that would have been too much.

For about a week, I hid the pain that was tearing me apart inside. All I wanted was to be accepted, to be loved, to be hugged and feel wanted. Was that too much to ask? Now, many years later, I often ask myself how many children are feeling the same thing?

The night-time routine of crying myself to sleep was making me insecure and scared to do anything in case I would be rejected for the slightest thing. One night it all got too much and I felt as if I wanted to die – and that's something no one should feel, especially a young child of nine. I felt that having those feelings of grief and sorrow were wrong and that somehow I was letting the side down in having such emotions. Yet enough was enough, I had to be with somebody.

I climbed stealthily out of my bed and remember to this day the chill I felt on my wet pyjama top as I crept out of the dormitory and climbed the stairs to Colley's room. I was terrified of being rejected and told off by Colley, but the inner pain was too much and I had to be with someone. I knocked on her door and she came out immediately, as she was still up. She took one look at my tear-stained face and I broke down sobbing uncontrollably, burying my face in her plump side. 'There, there,' she said. Colley had probably said the same thing to hundreds of weeping children over her years as a matron, yet for me at this hour of my greatest need, it was all I wanted to hear. Colley cuddled me, and as she sat me on her lap, spoke to me softly, explaining that everything would work out all right in the end. The next few months found me at Colley's door a few more times, but she was patient with me and helped me overcome my life's greatest crisis.

The half-term holiday was rapidly approaching, and Colin and I had nowhere to go. Whether the social services had mixed up the holiday dates I am not sure, but the O and A Centre was not available, as it was full up with other poor children suffering probably much more than us. Colley and Miss Sparrow, an older lady who helped with the evening duties of bathing and bedding down the young boarders, came to the rescue. It was decided that Colin would go with Miss Sparrow to her sister's house, a farm in Devon, and I would stay with Colley.

Colley lived opposite the school, in a fine modern house with her two older sisters, neither of whom had ever married. The sisters obviously knew about my situation and went overboard to spoil me, which I remember actually enjoying. Although Colley put on a tough exterior, she, too, made me more than welcome. I remember going with Colley up to Malvern, which seemed miles and miles away from the school, to visit Miss Hunt, the old headmistress of the school who had retired before I had first enrolled as a pupil. She was kind and gentle and I instantly took to her. The two ladies took me to Malvern common and I flew a kite that they had bought for me.

I remember one night in particular, feeling great anxiety gripping me, and having nightmares about my uncertain future. Such was my fear of the unknown and distress about the present that I wet the bed. I was very embarrassed about it when it was discovered the following morning. These two women were great. The sheets were off and in the washing basket and new clean linen placed upon my bed even before I had time to say sorry.

By the time the half-term break was over, I was getting used to the idea that I no longer had a regular family or a place that I could call home.

As I grew used to my new situation, I got on with life – after all, what else could I do at 10 years of age? Schooldays at Moyles Court were fun. The regime was pretty tough, but the hours spent in those lovely grounds made all the hours behind a desk doing maths worth it.

I was made the school postman – that was a fantastic job, because I got to ride the famous post bike, an old rickety thing that was held together by the rust. But more than that, I collected the mail from the office and distributed it to all the boarders. They all used to hold their breath as I walked into the room, every eye looking at me, hoping I would call out their name and hold out an envelope sent from home.

Every lunchtime, I would go to see to the school secretary, who would give me the outgoing mail. It was normally a bundle of brown envelopes, probably invoices to all the parents, held together with a thick elastic band. These letters were then put in a canvas satchel with a strap that went over my shoulder. I then had to cycle a mile down the road to the nearest post box. The highlight of the trip would be to ride over the ford in the stream running very close to the school. If the water level was high, it would come up to the pedals, and that was good fun. If it were low tide, I would cycle at full speed into the water and delight in the spray that was always refreshing during those long hot summer days.

Having the responsibility of being the postman was like being a Pony Express rider; if the weather was bad the mail still had to get through. Come floods or snow, the mail was always posted and always delivered faithfully to the children. Having the job was helpful, because nobody wrote to me and I guess no one thought to ask why I never had my name read out when the post was delivered. They probably all thought I had put my letters to one side, or had already read them because, after all, I was the postman.

Mount Everest

I spent much of my free time discovering the beautiful surrounds of the school. The jungle of undergrowth was amazing and there was no end to the trees I could climb. I remember the tallest tree by a climbing frame, a massive red cedar that was known to all as 'Mount Everest'. Only experienced tree climbers were allowed to climb that lofty peak, and then it was under strict supervision of a member of staff. You had to wear PE shorts and plimsolls, and also a jumper, because it got windy at the top!

First-termers were not allowed to climb Mount Everest, but from the moment I was told all the rules of the climb, the challenge rose in me. Only the best kids assailed those heights and I was determined to be among the elite number that had become legendary in the history of the school.

The first Saturday morning of the next term, I got my chance to become one of the few who could boast of climbing Mount Everest. I got permission and was inspected for dress and equipment before the ascent. A small group of children gathered at the bottom of the tree. The group normally grew in size the higher you climbed – the possibility of a fall probably generated more interest than a victor at the peak! The first branches were the worst: the gardener had cut away the lower limbs so younger children had no chance at all of starting the epic climb. In fact, if you could not master the first part of the tree, it was considered that you wouldn't have a chance later, and the climb would be abandoned in great embarrassment. I struggled and gritted my teeth as I tackled the first few feet. With grazed knees and scratched hands I looked up, and was single-minded in my quest to conquer Mount Everest. After what seemed to be all morning, I began to gain confidence and gain height as well. Soon I could see all over the grounds of the school, and the people below were like little ants scurrying around. The final few feet took my breath away as I realised that I had made it. Yes, I was 10 years old and I had climbed Mount Everest!

> *The final few feet took my breath away as I realised that I had made it. Yes, I was 10 years old and I had climbed Mount Everest*

The feeling of elation was hard to contain as I started the climb downwards. Yet contain it I must, because, in fact, the descent was worse than the ascent. My legs were by now scratched and bloodied, but as I dropped to the ground to the cheer of the crowd I wasn't concerned. After all, I was the returning hero, I was the conqueror and, for the moment, I had the limelight – and boy, didn't it feel good even if it lasted for only a few minutes!

Stupid Things

I did some daft and stupid things from time to time. One night during the summer term, when most of the younger children had gone in to be bathed and put to bed, I was on my own, as the other children of my age group were mainly girls and had already gone to the common room to play some game. I found my way into the old bike shed, which housed all the bikes belonging to the schoolchildren. It was beginning to get dark and the last warm rays of the setting sun settled on the tin roof, causing it to remain warm inside.

I discovered, in the fading light, as I was searching along one of the shelves reserved for the school caretaker, a tube of glue used for repairing punctures. On taking the lid off, and probably because the air wasn't ventilated well in the shed, I got a whiff of the glue's powerful, intoxicating vapours. These smells seemed to make me feel as if I was floating, yes even flying – a sensation I had never known before – and I actually enjoyed it.

Being something of an experimentalist, and with my head spinning, I rolled up a piece of scrap card and poured the glue down it. Then holding it instinctively as a cigarette, I had my first experience of 'getting high'.

Thinking about it now, it was no small miracle that I didn't die. Many times, young people experiment with glue and drugs and find – to the heartache of all concerned – that the first time is their last time – which is very sad.

I was completely 'out of it'. Talk about 'Lucy in the Sky with Diamonds'! I was rolling around on the dusty shed floor, high as a kite. I was totally intoxicated by the strong glue fumes, and when I finally managed to leave the shed, I collapsed again by the side of the swimming pool. Thankfully nobody saw me from the window and it was a secret that went with me when I left the school later. That was my first experience of being high, and it gave me a temporary release from the inner pain and emptiness that expressed its hunger more deeply each day.

Boarding school was the place where I discovered that girls were definitely different to boys, and could prove to be very interesting! Nancy was a gorgeous blonde, who was at that age when she, as I did, thought it very grown up to kiss. Although relationships at a preparatory school were very few and far between, Nancy and I struck up a friendship. It all started when our eyes met over the desks of a boring French lesson. Maybe it was the amorous language or the way I pronounced '*Je t'aime*', but she smiled at me and that was enough for me to write a love letter to her. Letters were exchanged across the classroom all afternoon, and when school was over and we had an hour of free time to fill before tea, we met up. The grounds afforded lots of shelter and so Nancy and I met up behind one of the rhododendron bushes.

> *It all started when our eyes met over the desks of a boring French lesson. Maybe it was the amorous language or the way I pronounced 'Je t'aime'*

The only problem was that she brought her best friend Vicky with her! That, although an embarrassment at first, soon proved to be a blessing for young love, as Vicky seemed to know all there was to know about kissing. Nancy and I kissed, but, according to Vicky, we got it all wrong. Apparently we had to use our tongues like the French people did. Well we used our tongues and discovered that was far more interesting. Then the moment came when we had to get more intimate: 'Show me yours and I'll show you mine' . . . the rest is censored!

Colley and the other night matrons didn't seem to notice that some of us boys were growing up. Stuart and I were developing a keen interest in the girls. Stuart was a year older than me and encouraged one particular girl to come to our two-bed dormitory and give us a striptease. The girl was from an African state, and was highly developed for 12 years of age, and the sight of her nude form did even more to fuel my interest in girls.

School was where I had my first proper girlfriend, Hazel Bodmin. Hazel was full of fun and, although not a stunner like Nancy, she was great to be with, and she liked nothing more than to take me into the locker room by the gym to sample the delights of continental kissing. Thankfully, it never went any further than that, but I'll always remember her as my first proper girlfriend.

I could write forever about my days at boarding school, but, once again, the sands of time were running out for me there. I was getting older, and so had to embark upon the next part of my journey into adulthood. This part of the journey would take me out of the beautiful surrounds of Moyles Court School and take me to Somerset, where my next school was located.

4

CHILDREN'S HOME KID

We had to go somewhere for the holidays. Kind as Colley
and Miss Sparrow were, the temporary arrangement of
half-term was never repeated. By now we had a new
social worker, another lady who said she knew all about
boys. I very much doubt she did, for she never seemed to
take any of my feelings into consideration when plans
were drawn up for my life. This social worker took Colin
and me to a children's home in Poole, Dorset. This was a
residential home which housed a maximum of twenty-
one children. We called the officer in charge Auntie Jenny.
A deputy and other staff assisted her. The staff worked
shifts, coming on in twos at 2 p.m. every afternoon and
working through by sleeping over on site till 2 p.m. the
next day. Auntie Jenny always seemed to be around, and
even if she was off duty you could usually find her in the
office with a mountain of paperwork.

The home was originally situated in an older property
not far from Poole Park, but the building fell into disre-
pair and I guess the council decided it was time for a pur-
pose-built home. This was good in the sense of having
amenities, but it did nothing for character, and the place,
although modern and called a children's home, was definitely not a home in any normal sense of the word. We

were welcomed as soon as we arrived and introduced to the staff on duty. Auntie Jenny gave us the guided tour and took us to a bedroom upstairs with three beds in it. By now I didn't mind dormitory life: in fact, I had got used to it, and a room to myself would have seemed strange. They felt it best to keep Colin and me together in a bid to help us settle in as quickly as possible. The other children were still at school and so we were able to familiarise ourselves with the layout of the home quietly. Then, one by one, the regular 'inmates' began to return from their day at school. First, the loud 'special needs' children who came by taxi (no wonder the social services say they have no money!), then the other children turned up, and once again we went through the interrogation process. This time it was nowhere near as bad as the boarding school experience, because these kids knew the system. They were like old lags, who taught us the ropes and what to watch out for. Nearly all of them had a horrific story of abuse and family break up to tell. We were all in the same boat, and so it was survival of the fittest. In this home no one was going to stop and listen to a sob story, for we all had one to tell.

Nearly all of them had a horrific story of abuse and family break up to tell

The children's home was a place of great discovery! A place where I learned much more about girls and sex, a place where I learned to shoplift, a place where I first got drunk and did many other crazy things. Incredibly I did all these things right under the noses of the staff, and, for the most part, they never confronted me or stopped me growing up the way that I had decided to. Inside me was a great emptiness, a feeling that there had to be more, a need to be loved and wanted. All these internal feelings fuelled the fire of the things that I would experience in the coming few years.

Girls!

I had been at the home for only a few nights. Each evening we would have to go through the bath-time ritual and, after scrubbing-up, we could go downstairs to watch telly, read or listen to records in the games room. Joss, a girl who was much older than me, was very friendly. She invited me to listen to records with her in the games room and I, thinking she looked good and was being nice to me, went along. The staff would be upstairs supervising the bath times and also putting the very young kids to bed. This left the whole ground floor wide open to anything, from kids smoking in the lounge (the designated smoking room for the 16+) to kids like me indulging in the forbidden fruits of the flesh. Joss soon had me dancing with her and before long we were kissing. The skills I had picked up from Nancy and Hazel paid off, and I passed as an experienced lover to Joss, who had been with boys before. Things soon got hot and we decided to meet later that night. Once I had gone to bed, the time seemed to take forever for Joss to come upstairs at her allotted bedtime. Her room was just across the corridor from my door and was set back a couple of feet from the main corridor. A gentle tapping on my door signalled she was ready to meet me.

What a risk we took, as we stood kissing against the wall of the children's home corridor. To be caught would have brought great trouble upon us, and probably all the staff of the home as well. As we stood in a passionate embrace, I lost my virginity. I am not proud of the way it happened, because it was the start of what would be a stronghold in my life, as I went from one partner to the next. Sex was easy at the home, and it seemed free at the time, but I paid for it later because it was the start of a slippery road that led to the depths of pornography, as I grabbed all the sex I could, in a bid to fill the great empty space in my life. I experimented with sex in many of the rooms of the home, and also in places in the grounds. The staff never seemed to see what was happening, and if they did, they chose not to say anything in order to have a quiet life.

Crime

Ben, an older lad who was about 15, used to take me to the shops in Parkstone on Saturday afternoons. He was bold and knew what he was doing. He was confident in his skills of shoplifting. The first time he took me with him stealing, we went into the Co-op supermarket. When we had walked around the shop he led me back out. I was puzzled, because he had told me he was going in there for chocolate, but he hadn't bought anything. When I questioned him about it he just laughed and showed me the contents of his pockets. Bar after bar of Cadbury's chocolate and other expensive delights appeared. My bulging eyes nearly popped out of their sockets. Ben told me never to tell anybody, and better still, promised to teach me all he knew. A real Fagin, he showed me how to look out for store detectives and store operatives, how to look like a proper shopper and not a teenage thief, how to fill your pockets with the best stuff and get it through the door without being caught.

Shane, a friend from the home, was of the same breed as me. He also wanted the good things and, not having the cash to pay for it, had the same option – go without, or steal it. Shane and I became the perfect crime partnership. We spent hours walking through the shopping centre in the centre of Poole acquiring all sorts of goodies our pocket money could never afford. The difficult problem wasn't in the stealing, but the explaining of how we found such bargains and bought so much with the rationed pocket money Dorset County Council gave us! We had all sorts of scams to make extra money.

One of the best, which always worked, was our begging trick. I would go up to a kindly-looking man or woman and with a pained, troubled look, I would ask for money, explaining that my brother was ill and I had no money to phone home. In those days, it would be two or five pence, and I had only to approach a few people in the crowded shopping mall and my income was supplemented very nicely.

The other easy cash trick was to fish for it! Yes, that's right, fishing. Not the type where you sit by a pond, but the kind where you roll up your sleeve and, in front of hundreds of people, drop a comb into the fishpond in the middle of the shopping centre. The pond had fish in it, but also the bottom was covered in money, coins thrown in for different charities. This trick took a certain cheek, as the whole thing had to look as if you had genuinely dropped something into the water. Then, in front of everyone, you had to fish out what you had 'accidentally' dropped, but along with the comb or whatever was dropped you also palmed a few of the coins from the bottom of the pond! The trick normally worked well and added a great deal extra to our pocket money. But when the arcade managers swept the coins into the centre of the pond things got more difficult. I remember being chased out of that arcade with a soaked and dripping arm on more than one occasion by security guards who spotted us illegally fishing!

One place that had a magnetic draw on me and the other baby bandits was the amusement arcade on Poole Quay. This arcade was alive with flashing lights, the sounds of sirens and bells going off continually, with pop music blaring in the background. This amusement arcade was the place to increase my cash: a get-rich-quick haven that was guaranteed, with one simple tool of the bandit's trade, the '*Star Wars* card'. *Star Wars* was the film of my early teens, and, of course, part of the obligatory merchandise was the bubble gum with collectors cards filled with images from the blockbuster of the decade.

What has a *Star Wars* card to do with getting money from the arcade? Simple – the arcade boasted some of the finest cascade machines I had ever set my eyes upon. For the uninitiated, cascade machines are the gambling machines with moving shelves that are heavily laden with coins – some with those high currency coins, the fifty-pence pieces of the early eighties. The shelves would go back and forth and the object of the gamble would be to drop a coin, usually a two-pence or five-pence piece, down a slot. If dropped at the right time, the coin would help to push money over the edge of the shelves as they went back and forth. Normally there were two shelves, and the honest punter, who would be lured by greed and what looked like easy money, would often lose his cash. At the start of the day, the arcade operators carefully placed the cash on the shelves, and it would take a lot of dropped coins to budge that build-up of overhanging coins. But the machine had one serious flaw, and we knew it.

The glass front where the coins were dropped upon the shelves had a gap that was just big enough for a *Star Wars* card to be inserted. Once correctly inserted, the *Star Wars* card did its job, sending coins cascading over the first shelf onto the second shelf. By now, the card would be back in your pocket out of sight, and as the money began to pour into the winning tray you had to look innocent and full of excitement, as you appeared to be a big winner! That *Star Wars* card trick earned me a small fortune.

It wasn't all success though, as I can still remember the pain as a size ten boot made sudden contact with my rear! I was slung out of the back door of that arcade a number of times and given a few 'lifetime' bans! The arcade was a good place for an opportunist thief as well. Shane and I would wait until a tourist – and there would be plenty of those – came into the arcade, and had placed their bags on the ground. Then, when the gaming machines gripped them, we struck by stealing anything that looked like it was worth a few pounds. Unfortunately, much of what we stole ended up at the bottom of the quay because we didn't have a 'fence' (somebody to sell stolen items to) at that time.

We had to make up a good excuse to go to town because any trip to town without money would look suspicious. So we became 'train spotters'! The railway line went right through the top of Poole High Street and, with level-crossing gates and a footbridge over the track, train spotting was the perfect excuse to get access to the shopping centre. Woolworths was only a few shops down from the level crossing and a prime target. Most of the staff at Woolworths were older, and the style and layout of the store afforded good cover for even an amateur shoplifter. I was into collecting model cars, as most boys of my age were, and Woolworths did an excellent line in replica model motorcycles! Those models were a piece of cake to take out of the presentation boxes and stuff into the coat pocket of my parka. By the end of the summer holiday, I had a whole collection of brightly coloured miniature motorcycles, and not only that, but a great boldness in my shoplifting skills.

Tesco was another shop like Woolworths, an easy hit for me. I guess I was a competent shoplifter in my teens, and Tesco was just another place to get what I wanted. I had acquired a taste for whisky and so would 'pick up' a small bottle every day. I would take my whisky into the Tesco in-store restaurant and brazenly pour some of it out into my coca-cola! I also regularly 'picked up' my new clothes from Tesco's home and wear department. My friend Shane would go one step further. Rather than do his washing, which we all had to do ourselves in the home, he would pick a whole change of clothes, changing his socks and underpants and leaving the dirty ones in the changing room!

The Undertakers and Juvenile Court

The walk into town always had short cuts, and one of those was behind some shops on the approach to Poole town centre. As we walked past the back of the different businesses, I would always slow down at the undertakers! Those gleaming hearses and sparkling limousines attracted my attention. What really intrigued me were the wooden boxes with flowers on top! Now one of those with wheels screwed to the bottom would make a fantastic go-cart! One Saturday morning, as we walked past the undertaker's garage, we noticed there was nobody about. Shane, Colin and I looked at each other, all knowing what the others were thinking. In a flash we were in the garage, hearts beating wildly, knowing this place was the place of the dead. Half expecting to bump into a zombie, we edged our way from the garage into the interior rooms. We only opened one door, probably because we were scared of being caught. That was the door to the chapel of rest! Shane and Colin went in, and as they passed through the doorway I gave them both a great big push that sent them crashing into an open coffin that had a rather grey-faced gentleman inside! I howled with delight, but they screamed in terror as they came face to face with their first corpse. I quickly slammed the chapel of rest door shut from the outside and held it tight, as Shane and Colin, who were desperate to get out, tried to pull the door open from the inside. My fun came to a swift end as I heard the undertaker, alerted by all the noise, shouting up the pathway at us. We ran as fast as we could from that place. I was laughing so much, though, I could hardly run at all and the other two threatened to beat me up because of what I had just done to them.

> *What really intrigued me were the wooden boxes with flowers on top. Now one of those with wheels screwed to the bottom would make a fantastic go-cart!*

We never did get the go-cart, but we did end those summer holidays in big trouble! Because we were all stealing and shoplifting together, sooner or later we were going to be caught. It came one afternoon as Auntie Jenny called us one by one into her office. The sight of this angry woman and her threats soon made me come clean about my criminal exploits, just as the others had already done before me. As we confessed to all we had been doing, the catalogue of crimes grew larger by the minute. Auntie Jenny had no choice but to call the police. We sat in the lounge looking glumly at the floor and ceiling, no one daring to speak, waiting for the police to arrive. When they finally came we all had to go one by one back into the office and make a statement. Most of the kids got off with a caution, but Shane, Colin and I had done so much we were charged and summoned to Poole Juvenile Court.

I don't think I really understood just how serious it all was. I will never forget this, my first court appearance. The chairman of the Juvenile Court, Mr Robertson, had a rounded balding head and a massive nose that looked like Concord in flight! The more I looked at him the more I laughed, to his obvious annoyance. Then, when he challenged me on violating the place of the dead and asked me why I did it, I couldn't contain my laughter. When I finally pulled myself together and told him I wanted to steal a coffin to make a go-cart, he hit the roof. I was given a severe warning but, thankfully, discharged. Shane, however, wasn't as lucky as Colin and me, for he was sentenced to six months in Borstal.

The Staff

On the whole, I think that the staff at the children's home were good people. Some seemed more caring than others and some seemed more terrifying. Uncle Harry was one that none of us messed with. He was in his forties and had worked in other places before he had settled into residential children's care. He did so only because his wife was the officer in charge. Uncle Harry was not a soft touch and always put on a hard-man image to staff and children alike. He would be outspoken and didn't care who he offended. He was not afraid of anything or anybody. He was a person who had done it all and liked everyone to know it! He would brag to us about the years he served in the army doing his National Service.

Meal times were an ordeal, and a living nightmare for any kid who hated to eat their vegetables. To be fair, the home always served up good food – not always what we wanted – but, nonetheless, good wholesome food using diet sheets that had been approved by the county council.

The dining room was large enough to have four tables, where six people could sit comfortably around each one. Once the two members of staff on duty had served the food, they would come and join us as we ate our meals. But Uncle Harry, who said he was brought up hard, couldn't stand the sight of one pea left on a plate. He would be furious if he saw a helping of cabbage or a Brussels sprout uneaten. He would be the enforcer! No one was going to waste food – not on his tour of duty. He would come up to the side of some poor quivering child and, taking their fork by force, would spear a sprout. Then, holding the fork about an inch from their eyes, he would say, 'If you don't eat this I'll ram it down your throat!' What child is going to argue with such bullying? Uncle Harry meant what he said. If force were needed, he would use it, and not minimum force either. I saw him use force on others, and there were times when he was happy to use it on me as well.

'If you don't eat this I'll ram it down your throat!'

You never knew where you were with Uncle Harry. Just when you thought you knew him, something would happen and you realised how wrong you were. If we were pillow-fighting in our dormitory, you could guarantee it would be Uncle Harry who would stealthily creep upon us like a commando and crack our heads together.

The man instilled fear in most of us, and that fear caused us to creep around him. We would ask the staff who was going to be on the next shift, and would shiver as if someone had walked over our graves when they said Auntie Jenny and Uncle Harry. I can remember times when Auntie Jenny would get the wrong end of the stick as she waded in to sort out disputes among the children. As the innocent party protested the truth, Uncle Harry would come in heavy-handed and 'quieten' any resistance. Even when Uncle Harry had a day off, we would only sigh in relief as his Ford Cortina cruised up the drive and away from the children's home. I laugh now as I can hear the petrified warning shouts resounding around the home, as some kid spotted his car returning from a trip out!

The children's home staff were always strict – I guess they had to be – and none of them ever gave in or showed any real affection to any one of us. It was probably forbidden for the staff to really love us and to show it by an occasional hug. But a hug and some loving affection was what we wanted more than anything else in the whole world. Many of us had been rejected, even discarded like surplus property by our parents. All we wanted was love. The county council fulfilled its duty *in loco parentis*, but duty was all it was. The regulations and the system prevented us from starving or even being abused by bad parents. However, it never fulfilled our greatest need, to be loved and to be able to give love.

> *A hug and some loving affection was what we wanted more than anything else in the whole world*

Uncle Owen came to the home one Sunday afternoon. He was a small man with blonde hair, a big bushy blonde moustache and a great big smile that won your heart immediately. Uncle Owen was a radical. I didn't realise it until years later, but he was a challenge to the system that was cold and unfeeling. He wanted us to laugh, to be able to talk freely about the pain inside and to be able to enjoy ourselves. For hours he would talk to us and write poems about us that would make us laugh and smile. He would champion our causes and didn't flinch in the face of Uncle Harry. Uncle Harry couldn't stand this ray of hope and sunshine that had suddenly lit the dark recesses of the home. The two of them were never on duty together. I think if that had ever happened there would have been sparks and bloodshed, for Uncle Owen would not have put up with Uncle Harry's table manners! Uncle Owen was with us for the summer holiday period, and as fast as he came, he went again. We all kept asking questions about Uncle Owen's strange disappearance, and although no official reason was given, one of the lady members of staff told us that there was a conflict of understanding in disciplinary matters concerning the care of children. The bottom line was that Uncle Owen had challenged the hierarchy of the home, his love and forward thinking had threatened their security and so a campaign had been mounted to remove him. Sadly it had been successful.

I met Uncle Owen years later walking down Poole High Street, and when we recognised each other, what a hug we had in front of everyone. He was genuinely pleased that I had survived my time at the home. We never met again, but that one meeting was enough for us both to remember.

There was one member of staff who also sticks clearly in my mind. Auntie Janet was a pretty-faced young woman who I first saw when she came for a job interview one afternoon. She had been to college and was trained for children's care. She impressed the interview board and so she got the job. Auntie Janet seemed different to the others – she didn't smoke, swear or smile at anything smutty. Her father was the minister of the Broadstone United Reformed Church, although she never verbally confessed her faith, which was probably something she was forbidden to do, particularly to young, impressionable children. Auntie Janet was quiet and always fair when trying to arbitrate during heated debates among the children. She never lost her cool or shouted like the other staff, and yes, the more I think about it, there was certainly something different about her.

I wonder if she was a Christian? Certainly by the way she lived, I would say today she probably was. I like to think, also, that she prayed for us kids. She would have seen hurting children longing to be loved and accepted. She would have known the Saviour's feelings for children: how he loved them and hugged them, picked them up and blessed them and scolded the disciples when they tried to keep the kids away. Jesus knew the simplistic faith of a child and said, 'Don't stop them! For the kingdom of heaven belongs to such as these', as the kids pushed past the strong ex-fishermen to jump on Jesus' lap.

Years later, at the 1996 Assemblies of God conference, where I was ordained as a minister, I met one of the ladies who had spent her childhood at the home. As my wife and I drank a cup of tea in our chalet at Bognor Regis, we listened as she told us of others from the home who had been saved by the grace of God. I can still see her face now, smiling as we remembered those painful, hurting days of our youth. The joy of Jesus was indeed her strength, for she, too, could write a book about being set free from the kingdom of darkness. We talked of Auntie Janet and wondered whether she prayed for us all. If she had prayed for us, as we guessed she did, then she, too, would rejoice with us. For out of all of those kids at the home during our time there, five are now Christians and enjoying God's love and healing power in their lives. We hugged each other as we parted, praising God that we had come through and now possessed the greatest life in the world through Jesus Christ, who loved us and gave himself for us.

5

THE KINGDOM OF DARKNESS

First Impressions

The day I went with a social worker to view the new boarding school, it rained. Colin was not with us, as it was decided by the social services that he needed to be placed in a special educational needs school. There was such a school in Poole, so Colin remained at the children's home. Maybe the rain was an omen that I wouldn't be happy at this next school. As the car sped through the Somerset roads, we approached Yeovil, and the social worker, a man whose name I can't remember, began to give me a briefing about trying to create a good impression to all the people I would soon be meeting. During the last few miles of the trip I felt sick. I had always suffered from travel sickness, but maybe it was more than the motion of the car – maybe it was also a feeling of dread as I was once again facing the unknown.

I was breathing in deeply as we turned off the main road into the school grounds. A farm building on one side of the road and an old church on the other, made the entrance to the school look mysterious yet impressive. The school had great big gates that, once passed through, gave view to a fabulous-looking manor house with ivy growing up the walls, giving an aged but magnificent appearance. The drive circled round past the front porch creating a grass roundabout island with a flagpole in the middle. That certainly impressed me, but what really grabbed me was the Sea Venom fighter jet parked on the grass and the two anti-aircraft gun emplacements. I didn't want to speak to any teachers now: instead I wanted to explore all the exciting things at the front of the school. My social worker was firm and insisted that we get on with the business of meeting the headmaster.

The doorbell was rung, and after what seemed ages, a tall and somewhat overweight man with incredibly bushy eyebrows appeared. This was the headmaster, and he soon made us feel welcome as he shook our hands and asked us to follow him. We went through the front door, a privilege that I was seldom allowed in the future, as it was forbidden for pupils to use it. The main hall was quite awe-inspiring, the prominent feature being a grand wooden staircase with elaborate carvings. The walls were filled with original paintings of people from the past who had probably lived in the house over the years it had stood.

As we followed the headmaster into his office – a place that I would learn to try to keep out of – we passed a gun case containing all sorts of rifles locked safely away. All these images flashed through my mind and I thought to myself that maybe this wouldn't be such a bad place after all. After a short chat, in which the headmaster spelled out a brief history of the school and its involvement with the Royal Navy through the Sea Cadets, I was asked to do a short test. The questions didn't look official, but I guess they wanted to know how intelligent I was and what they would be taking on!

Once the test was over, the guided tour began. We saw a dormitory, the classrooms, school library, the many playing fields and a large gymnasium. The swimming pool was looking green, but some excuse was given for its strange colour and also a reassurance that it would be ready for use by the time I started at the school!

The tour took a long time and I should have remembered the last tour at Moyles Court when I was only shown the 'best bits' of the school! But the sight of all those guns and the aeroplanes parked on the grass thrilled me and then there was the school's own stream and water mill with a deep pool filled with eels. Even better, it had its own fire station, fully equipped with uniforms and a vintage Dennis fire engine.

This was all too much for a young boy, and so I was hooked! By the time we shook hands with the headmaster and his wife, it had been agreed that I would be starting at the school as a new pupil in the coming autumn term.

> *This was all too much for a young boy, and so I was hooked!*

September soon came around and once again the car carrying me sped through the Somerset roads. This time my suitcase was in the boot, loaded with my new uniform. The uniform was pretty good for the young boys enrolling at the school – black trousers and an army jumper complete with epaulettes. The girls wore the same jumpers, but had black leather trousers or skirts, which apparently had won an award in the past for the 'most practical school uniform'.

The Lords of Discipline

The school had a system of discipline with much of the authority delegated to older pupils who had three ranks – head boy and head girl, prefects and aides. I was to discover very quickly, to my terror, that these ruling pupils ran the school once the academic day was over. They organised shower times, enforced bedtimes and dished out punishments called 'defaulters' to anyone they chose.

The aides had a small common room not far from the main hall and stairway of the school. Walking past the door of that common room was very risky, as the door would often be slightly ajar and just as you thought you had slipped by unnoticed someone would shout out your name. Once your name was called you had no choice but to obey! The common room door would be promptly shut and torture would be the menu of the day, from crushed hands to red ears and noses.

One day, as I crept along the corridor, I was summoned into the common room and interrogated about something that someone else was supposed to have done. Because my answers were not what they wanted to hear, the five aides in the room ordered me to stand in front of the dartboard. Then, as I stood in absolute terror, they began to play 'Around the Clock'. I begged them to stop, but what was a 12-year-old boy to five young men between 17 and 19? To make matters worse, they demanded that I keep my eyes open. The fear of losing my sight was real and I had a job to control my bladder. Mercifully, my ordeal ended as one of them threw his dart wildly and it missed the board lodging itself deep in my leg below my knee instead! Because the tears started flowing down my cheeks they released me, and although blood oozed from the fresh wound, I counted myself lucky to be alive and to come out

> *Although blood oozed from the fresh wound, I counted myself lucky to be alive and to come out of that hellhole in one piece*

of that hellhole in one piece, as others had suffered much worse at the hands of those cruel bullies.

The school, although good academically, was hopeless at after school supervision. Because of this, I was exposed to all sorts of things no young teenager should face. I became a nasty person as I grew up: uncaring, cold, selfish, filthy-tongued and perverse in many ways. I can't blame my wrongdoings on anyone else: as the Bible clearly says, we all have to give an account for our own lives. Yet I can't help but think that the school had helped turn me into an evil, cold, scheming crook who would go on from that place to bring misery, not only to myself, but also to the lives of many other people.

Although I had quickly picked up many scams, things didn't always go to plan! I will never forget the day a little scheme of mine backfired badly. The school always had afternoon games at least twice a week and, not being keen on cross-country running or wanting to donate a copious supply of blood on the rugby field, I would bunk off with a couple of mates. In the summer, we would go and climb a tall tree at the end of the school grounds. Sitting in the lofty branches, we would enjoy a quiet smoke and watch the other lads doing athletics, sweating in the heat of the day. During the winter, we would slip into the changing rooms after all the other lads, who had stood in the yard for roll call, ran off to the sports event of their choice. As the thundering rumble of football boots on concrete faded away we would laugh at the others playing barbaric games on the frozen rugby pitch, while we lit up our cigarettes in the warmth of the shower room.

On one particular Wednesday afternoon, a visiting rugby team came to play an inter-schools match with a trophy at stake. It was a freezing day and so, as always, we quietly slipped into the changing room area as all the others went to the field to cheer on the home side. We lit up our cigarettes, but were troubled when we heard Mr Shorthand talking to somebody in the yard outside. Once he had gone, we darted into the school library. Although we couldn't smoke in there, at least it was warmer than the freezing rugby pitch!

At the end of the match, as everyone came in from the fields, we slipped out of the library and joined the crowd as if we had been with everyone all the time. It all seemed a perfect plan. It had always worked so well. Suddenly, a cry came from the visiting school team's changing room. A lad had been robbed! Fifteen pounds had been taken from his wallet left in his trouser pocket. Now this had brought great shame upon the school. The headmaster was furious and instructed the 'Lords of Discipline' to seek out the perpetrator of such a scandalous crime.

The head boy immediately made initial inquiries, and by teatime had established that I, along with about six others, was absent from the rugby match. One by one we were summoned to the infamous aides' common room. Trembling, I stood before the head boy and had to give my sorry account of bunking off. The problem for me was that I had actually been in the vicinity of where the cash was stolen. It looked pretty bad for the others and me as we all protested our innocence to a kangaroo court that needed a scapegoat.

The days that followed were an absolute nightmare for a boy of 12. The teachers must have seen something or heard on the grapevine that severe bullying was going on, but nothing was done to protect the weak and vulnerable younger children from the hands of the vicious older pupils. The Lords of Discipline were under increasing pressure to reveal the identity of the thief. The honour of the school was at stake, and if they couldn't produce the culprit by the end of the autumn term, the school's Christmas party was under the threat of cancellation. I can still remember the nights I was interrogated by the prefects. The terror of those nights haunted me for years afterwards. My dormitory was at the end of an ancient wine cellar corridor. To get to the dormitory and the toilet and washbasin area, you had to go through the long, dark wine cellar.

In those nights of terror, I would be woken by the sound of many marching hobnailed boots crashing down on the cellar floor, getting louder and louder as they drew closer to the dormitory. With a loud bang the door would be kicked open, almost coming off its hinges. Practically wetting myself with fear as I cowered in bed, the aides and prefects would drag me screaming from my bed. All the other lads in the room knew I was going to get a severe beating, but they were too petrified to raise any objection to the horrific interrogations. I would be thrown against the wash area wall, where they would take turns each night to lead the questioning. I was kicked in the groin so many times, I am amazed that I survived and have been able to experience the joy of being a dad. The sickening pain and the vomiting, as a size ten hobnailed Sea Cadet boot crashed into my testicles, is something I shall never forget.

Night after night, they thought up some new torture to extract a confession from me, just to satisfy the headmaster. They filled a washbasin with water and held my face under the water until I nearly drowned. Then, when I refused to confess to a crime I didn't commit, they would swear at me, holding sharp penknives under my throat. My blood would freeze as they threatened to cut me and slice the flesh off my bones. One night, a cigarette lighter was used to burn the side of my face. As the pain became unbearable I sobbed, but the sound of a pitiful young boy in abject fear didn't move their callous hearts. Once, when they had kept up the torture for a week, the sound of their boots along the corridor didn't wake me. But a starting pistol fired right by my face did. My hearing was impaired for days afterwards, and I had a black grease burn mark down the side of my face. To my despair, not one teacher inquired as to why my face was injured. Not one teacher observed the way I cowered around the grounds and walked in terror in the school building.

My blood would freeze as they threatened to cut me and slice the flesh off my bones

One day, the boy who stole the money revealed himself to me. He was about 16 years old and much bigger than I was, and to protect him he shall remain nameless. He actually boasted to me that he committed the crime and said that I was going to take the blame for him! Early one morning before breakfast he told me to follow him into the exercise yard. As I went through the door he had passed to go outside, he turned on me, placing a well-aimed fist straight in my young face. I was on the floor with blood spurting from a near broken nose and stars before my eyes. He informed me that that was just for starters, unless I confessed to the theft of the fifteen pounds. I hated him for that. The pain was dreadful, but as I picked myself up off the floor, I vowed I would get even with this big bully.

The next day I went to the school fire station and climbed into the driving seat of the vintage fire engine. Stealing the ignition keys, I took them outside and threw them into the bushes. Then, getting a tube of glue, I squirted the adhesive over the seats of the appliance. I let down all the tyres of the fire engine and finally grabbed an axe from inside the cab, which I took round to the science laboratory and sent it crashing through the window. I left the devastation that I had caused in the fire station and went looking for the headmaster. When I found him I asked him if I could have a private word in his ear, to which he agreed. I told him the name of the bully who had punched me and stolen the fifteen pounds, and explained that I had seen that lad messing around in the fire station and that I was worried that he would blame something else on me. The headmaster told me I had done the right thing in going to him and he would keep this information confidential. As I watched him stroll over to the fire station, I knew that my plan was going to work. Sure enough, that very day, the bully's parents were summoned to the school. The lad got a good caning, and by that evening had been expelled. I never saw him again, nor did I want to. None of the younger lads liked him, as he would steal from them. He was a vicious, bullying thug, and I thought that my day's work was in the best interests of all. The beatings stopped from that very day, as everyone quickly learned that the expelled bully was the real culprit.

I should have learned my lesson from the theft of the fifteen pounds about being in the wrong place at the wrong time. But I always seemed to learn the hard way, unfortunately, through my own stupid mistakes and not someone else's. Jack, my school friend, and I decided it would be fun to go into Yeovil one afternoon, rather than going for the obligatory cross-country run. Once we had lined up in PE kit for roll-call and the directions for the run were given, everyone was off. However, Jack and I went straight back into the changing room and dressed in our weekend clothes; we were going to hit the town! Once dressed, we walked out through the school gates and waited on the main Yeovil road. Presently a car came round the bend and we flagged it down. The couple inside were going into town and were only too pleased to give us a lift.

As Jack and I walked through Yeovil's busy shopping streets, we laughed to each other as we thought of our exhausted schoolmates gasping for air as they completed the cross-country run. We had a cigarette and bought a burger from Wimpy – this was the life! Then, as we walked up to the bus stop to see if we could catch a ride back to somewhere near the school, disaster struck. Mr Banton, head of maths at the school, was heading our way down the high street. We turned in our steps and darted into a side street, but it was too late, as he had seen us.

Knowing that we had probably been spotted, and that the punishment for being absent without leave was a caning, we started back to the school. When we got back, Mr Evans met us. He was a hard Welshman who delighted in exacting discipline upon wayward boys. He informed us that we were in big trouble and were to report immediately to the headmaster's quarters. Jack and I knew all too well that the cane was going to make an appearance, so we darted up the back stairs to our dormitory. As quick as we could, we pulled on about four pairs of pants each, hoping that the padding would soften the blows from the caning.

Sure enough, we were told to go into the headmaster's lounge and to bend over. One, two, three . . . yes, six times that cane came down across my backside, and although the extra pants helped, the pain was still very real! When the headmaster got his breath back, he told us to go and report back to Mr Evans. We knocked on Mr Evans' door and he bellowed out that we were to enter. Standing in front of him, he ripped into us verbally that we were scum in dishonouring the school by avoiding the cross-country run and then hitching a lift to Yeovil right outside the school gates. Once he had finished the torrent of abuse, he smacked us both in the mouth, and told us if we ever did anything like that again we would be expelled and he would see to it personally that our feet wouldn't touch the ground.

The school was a typical English boarding school, where the men would be trained to sort out their differences like 'gentlemen'! A boy named Harris, a troublemaker who was two years older than me, started a fight with me one day in the wine cellar. I wasn't particularly violent and didn't go looking for fights either, but when this red-haired lad picked on me I wasn't about to let him walk over me, so I stood my ground. In the cramped space of the wine cellar we began to throw punches and instantly a crowd gathered, baying for blood. When a struggle broke out, and it often did, the younger pupils would dash around the school like African messengers shouting out 'Fight, fight'. Everyone would stop what they were doing and come to watch what would usually be a good, unofficial, sporting spectacle.

I didn't think that I stood much chance against Harris, as he was older, taller and heavier. But I was holding my own and, to the delight of the onlookers, had drawn blood from the side of his mouth, which enraged him all the more. Such was the frenzied shouting of the spectators that the PE and science teacher, Mr Thomas, came along and, with his strong, long arms, quickly separated us. 'Follow me,' he commanded, as he walked out of the school to the gymnasium. We followed him, and so did a vast crowd of schoolchildren eager to see more action. Once at the gymnasium, we went inside and the door was shut to everyone else: they had to be content with peeping through the windows. Mr Thomas tossed a pair of old boxing gloves to each of us and then told us to get on with it! After a few short rounds, both of us were wiping blood from our sore, bruised noses. By the fifth round we were exhausted, and so the match was declared a draw and we were told to shake hands. I never fought with Harris again after that day. We had developed a respect for each other and, later on, actually stood up for each other in times of conflict.

Sea Cadets

The school prided itself on its Royal Navy connections. The deputy head, Mr Shorthand, was an ex-Royal Navy fitness and drill instructor, and didn't we know it! Every Tuesday afternoon was allocated to the Sea Cadets, something that I had thought sounded good at first, but learned later to dread and loathe. In my eyes, Sea Cadets was just a good excuse for the aides and the teachers, who doubled up as officers, to bully us and make men out of us. They might have meant well, but it was sheer misery, as most of us hated the drills and all the spit and polish that went with it.

Parades were the things I hated most. It meant hours of getting your uniform ironed correctly and for a young lad that was hard work. When I sat spitting and polishing my parade boots, they never seemed to come up to a shine as they were supposed to, and when they finally did shine, some sadistic older boy would normally stand on them just as we lined up for inspection.

On one parade, we were told that Commander Tricky of the Royal Navy would be giving us a General

Inspection. This man apparently organised the drill cere-
mony for Lord Mountbatten's military funeral. He was a
fussy man and everything had to be absolutely perfect.

The drill practice got so boring, and every time I lifted
that old 303 rifle it seemed to get heavier. Until we got the
order 'general salute – present arms' correct, we would
have to keep on doing it. I think it was exhaustion and
nerves fraying due to all the threats of violence if we didn't
perform well that finally made me crack. The drill officer
came up to me in the line and began to bark right in my face
all the horrible things he was going to do to me. This was
the straw that broke the camel's back and before I could
help myself I shouted a load of abuse back to the bullying
officer. That was it! An example had to be made and I was
going to be the cadet who would be publicly disciplined.

I was marched, in disgrace, to the front of the building,
where most of the cadet force were doing different drills
like knot-tying and gun assembly. The Commanding
Officer, Mr Shorthand, was talking to the headmaster, and
when he was informed of my insubordination, adminis-
trated instant discipline by ordering me to run around the
roundabout grass island in front of the school with the
303 rifle held high above my head. This gave the rest of
the school some comic relief. All their eyes were now
upon me, as not many had dared to defy the powers that
be. The gun was too heavy for me and by the time I had
run about four times around the grass roundabout my
energy was completely drained. I stumbled back in front
of the senior officers and the headmaster. This time
enough was enough, I didn't even care if they expelled
me. So, in anger, this 12-year-old boy flung the rifle down
at their feet, shouted an obscenity (too rude for printing!)
and stormed off. Maybe it was because of my age, maybe
because they realised they had pushed this sailor too far,

but to my amazement nobody followed me. By the time I had walked off my anger and returned to the building a few hours later, it was all forgotten by the adults. That night I was the hero of my dormitory as the lads relived the expression on old Shorthand's face as the rifle I had flung in anger came crashing down at his feet!

Sea Cadets also meant lots of sailing on Sherborne Lake. I hated those afternoons of waterborne activities. Sailing was so boring and left me feeling frustrated. We did all the hard work, while the officer would shout out orders like 'go about'. If you didn't respond quickly enough, the voyage became a misery, as the older cadets would hit us and threaten us with more violence once we got back to school.

If sailing was a bad memory, then my rowing escapades were a nightmare! The coxswain would shout out his orders to the poor shipmates that had to row up and down the lake. With blisters on our hands, we sat on the wet seats of the boat and struggled with those huge, heavy oars. When the order was given to 'ship oars' we would have to take them out of the water and hold them upright in the boat. The cold water would run down our arms, soaking our tops and making the time on the water all the more miserable. I don't think any of my schoolmates enjoyed those afternoons. We endured them, longing for the time we would be ordered off the water and told to get on the school bus for the short trip back to the school.

The Kingdom of Darkness

I was unhappy and, like most people living without God, I felt empty inside. At that time I never had any thoughts about God. I guess the spiritual hunger I felt had to be satisfied, but because of my natural tendency to do wrong, I

satisfied it not with the love, peace and joy God offers
through his son Jesus Christ, but through the dark powers of the occult. The school had all sorts of teenagers
boarding, from many different backgrounds. Through
such diversity of thinking, occult ideas were given to me.

I would visit the school library and spend hours of my
free time reading the books in the supernatural section. I
filled my mind with Satanism, which Dennis Wheatley
had so freely written about. I read
and re-read his books, longing to
taste the dark powers of Satan
myself. I took great pleasure in
reading his obligatory warning at
the front of each of his books, that
'the occult is of a real and dangerous nature'. I found myself often
drawing satanic symbols and
designing Ouija boards, using

The occult is of a real and dangerous nature

those same ancient occult symbols I had seen in those old
library books.

The school was, as I mentioned earlier, right by an old
farmhouse and an ancient church with a graveyard. The
farmhouse boasted a gruesome relic from the days of the
English Civil War. The relic was a human skull, which
had belonged to a Theophilus Broome, a supporter of
Oliver Cromwell. On being wounded he had escaped the
battlefield on his horse and made his way to his family's
home, which was the old farmhouse. The wounded sol-
dier was losing blood and his fight for life. With his dying
breath he gasped his last request to his sister and onlook-
ing family. He begged them to sever his head from his
torso and bury it separately from his body, so that the
Royalist men would not take his head and display it
impaled on a pole as an example to other sympathisers to

Cromwell's cause. The dying man then uttered a blood-curdling curse upon any who should meddle with his skull or try to bury it with his body. When Theophilus Broome died, the family carried out his dying wishes by severing his head from his body. The body was buried in the churchyard, but the head was placed in a wooden box, which was hidden in the wall above the dining room door in the old farmhouse.

From time to time, people had tried to remove the gruesome skull and bury it in the churchyard, but every time this was attempted something bad would happen to the persons involved. One man actually died while in the process of burying the skull, when a falling roof slate from the church hit him on the head.

The family living in the old farmhouse believed in the curse and, although they talked freely about the skull, they also always treated the whole thing with great respect. Sometime before I went to the school, a television reporter and crew went to make a story about the skull. A researcher with the crew picked up the skull and mocked the whole idea of the curse. Later, after filming, the crew went home. The researcher drove in a separate car, but never reached home as he had an accident on the motorway and was killed.

Once, when I went to the old farmhouse with another lad to hear about the skull, the box was lowered down and placed open on a table in the hallway. The telephone rang and the farmer left us while he answered it. Because of its dark and macabre history, I just had to touch the skull. Much to the horror of my friend I placed my hands upon the dark relic of Theophilus' cranium. I didn't feel anything. I should have been scared to delve into the powers of darkness, but, such was my unhealthy interest in the occult, I had lost my in-built fear of what goes bump in the night. All these tales of curses and the undead fuelled my hunger for the supernatural. One Saturday night I went to the churchyard along with three other boys, and when we found the headstone of Theophilus Broome, attempted to hold a séance. We held hands around the headstone and, as we called upon the powers of the spirit world, the wind began to blow in the darkness of the churchyard. The clouds blocking out the light of the moon added to the atmosphere. The headstones formed dark shapes that looked threatening, as if they were figures surrounding us in our morbid quest to contact those long dead. The wind swept around us and, although no one saw or heard anything, I sensed a real and tangible presence of evil that sent a shiver down my spine.

> *We held hands around the head-stone and, as we called upon the powers of the spirit world, the wind began to blow in the darkness of the churchyard*

The skull story fascinated me, but it didn't satisfy my lusting for occult power. Dennis Wheatley and other authors had painted this picture in my immature, impressionable mind that there was real power to be had in following the dark lord, Lucifer. I actually believed Satan would reward me with supernatural abilities if I gave myself over to him.

From the moment I saw the tarot cards, I knew that fortune-telling was something I could do. A lad who also had a great interest in the occult brought a deck of tarot cards back to school with him. Some of the boys in our dormitory thought it a laugh, but for me it was more: this was a serious business to investigate. This deck of cards could bring joy or sorrow and even fear to people. I looked upon it as an expression of the power I believed Satan had given me. I stole some money from a tuck box to buy the cards from the lad. Once they were in my hands, I began to call upon Satan, asking him to empower me more than ever. I would read the cards for different people in the school, and they would be amazed as I would explain through the cards their past experiences and what emotions they were feeling at that time. They would gasp as I revealed their future to them.

I enjoyed the power of fortune-telling in the beginning, as it gave me a sense of excitement. But, although I had tasted forbidden dark powers, it didn't satisfy my hungry heart. I read the cards for a few years and learned also to read palms, which was a little more challenging. I really had called on Satan and believed I had the gift for such things in the supernatural. One rainy Saturday afternoon, as I talked with a boy slightly older than myself about my experiences with the occult, he asked me if I had ever tried astral projection. I had read about this eastern practice, but had not yet tried it out. We talked about the benefits of this different kind of supernatural experience and read that Alistair Crowley, the infamous Satanist and mystic, had often practised the out-of-body experience called astral projection.

That was it! I had to add it to my dark repertoire of occult experiences. We slipped up the back staircase to our third-floor dormitory. As we lay on our beds, we meditated for hours on the 'third eye', the one that the mystics say we have. I remember being disappointed, as nothing seemed to happen. It was that afternoon I called on Satan quietly but determinedly and asked him to give me his power.

The dark seed, though, had been planted. To my surprise, some nights later in the small hours, I had this incredible experience: an experience over which I didn't seem to have any control. Whether it was a dream or a supernatural reality created by the dark evil forces of satanic deceit I don't know, but the whole astral projection experience was real. Describing it now, years later, all I can say is that there was an inner struggle, where I was almost fighting for breath and freedom, then, suddenly I was liberated from the confines of my physical body. I had this fantastic sensation of flying. The flying I could control and, as I soared upwards and banked, the whole experience seemed real. I had many such out-of-body adventures, where I would be in places where I could see people and hear what they were saying, but somehow they couldn't see me. The concept of flight fascinated me and I enjoyed it as it was happening.

The scary bit was returning to my body. Now that was frightening, as I seemed to return at such a speed that my whole body would jump like a heart patient being resuscitated by electric shock, almost to the point of falling out of the bed! From the moment of asking Satan for the power to project my body on another plane, to the point when I became a Christian, I had many such astral flights. They became a normal part of my life. Although the experiences were both exhilarating and scary at the same time, they never gave me peace or a lasting feeling of satisfaction.

I wish now that someone had taken me to one side at the beginning of my teenage years and told me all that I was looking for could be found in Jesus Christ. Yes, a life given to him in return would be filled with joy and satisfaction that no pen or tongue could fully tell. Alas it was not to be, and so my quest continued in the murky waters of satanic deceit. I was Satan's willing servant and there was much more of his evil to enter me before I would finally see the light of truth that would set me totally free.

To write more about my search for dark powers would only glorify Satan. In this book I have been open and honest in writing it all as it was. This is not to focus your attention upon the Prince of Darkness, but rather to turn your eyes upon the King of Kings and Lord of Lords whose name is Jesus Christ – Jesus Christ who overcame this world, sin and the devil by the mighty power and triumph of his cross.

The things I recollect have now been forgiven and forgotten by God, but I have written them so that you may comprehend how totally lost my soul was and the captivity that a child as young as I found myself in.

Maybe, as you are reading this now, you are thinking of some child you know, for there are many young children who are in the grip of Satan's vice-like claws. As you think of these child captives, take hope in God. The deliverance that he gave me, he can also give to others. Through prayer, you too can see prisoners such as I was gloriously set free.

Drugs and Drink

The child boarders brought back all sorts of contraband from abroad as they returned from their school holidays. Alex, my mate whose dad was working in India, brought back a great selection of cannabis resin. As soon as he saw me, as he carried his bags up the school's back stairs, he began to tell me of his holiday exploits: the drugs, drink and, of course, the sexual conquests.

That night, in the dormitory, a big 'joint' was rolled up and, as we stood smoking it by the window looking at the stars, my head was swimming. Those short periods of being high temporarily obliterated my inner feelings of insecurity and pain. One of the side-effects of cannabis is laughing, and one of the lads, a tall boy called Flanders, was completely gone, buzzing away and out of control, laughing his head off. This was funny, but it soon wore off as one of the teachers who lived in private quarters in the main house came flying up the stairs in his dressing gown, awakened by the raucous laughter.

Thankfully, I leapt a world record jump over three beds, and managed to get under the covers just as the door flew open! The sight of the teacher standing in the doorway soon brought me back down to earth, but Flanders always went too far and, although he had made it back to his bed like the rest of us, he couldn't suppress his laughter. That, and the smell of the drugs, was a give-away. The teacher asked the dorm leader, a lad called Mark who was pretending to be asleep, who had been smoking drugs? Mark, who was pretty convincing as a roused sleeper, pretended that he didn't know what was going on. The teacher was after blood and threatened to put us all on 'defaulters'. This made Flanders finally confess to the teacher, not to smoking drugs, but to the lesser crime of cigarette smoking. The next day Flanders appeared before the headmaster and, after a lecture on the dangers of smoking, received six of the best and was also told that if he was involved in any more escapades with cigarettes he would be expelled.

Smoking was a regular habit for about half the school. It was forbidden but, as the cigarettes were easy to obtain, children as young as 12, like myself, were hooked. Obtaining dope was a little more difficult, but as long as you were willing to pay, you could buy as much dope as you liked. I didn't have much money, except for the times when I stole it from other people. However, all was not lost, as I had a good friend nicknamed Curly, who not only had finance, but a regular supplier and so was able to feed his drug habit every week. Curly was probably

my best friend at that time and was happy to share his
drugs with me free of charge! The amazing thing was that
Curly's supplier was actually one of the school's full-time
teachers!

Many a weekend was spent lazing around the shower
rooms 'floating' on the effects of 'Black Leb' or 'Moroccan
Gold'. When drugs were not available, the next best thing
we used to slip out of reality was alcohol. Obtaining
booze was a real adventure and there were two main
sources. One was to buy it illegally and smuggle it back
into the school after a day trip to the largest and nearest
town, which was Yeovil: the other was to steal the headmaster's private supply!

The latter was something I got pretty adept at over a
period of a few months. The headmaster's office, the
place I had my first interview, doubled up as a private
dining room. Among the antique furniture was a side-
board laden with a full decanter of burgundy. Jack, who
was a good friend, and I, discovered the burgundy one
day by chance when we were asked to take, unaccompa-
nied, some boxes of books to the headmaster's office. We
both drank a mouthful from the decanter. The deep red
liquid burned and glowed as it flowed into our mouths.
We looked at one another with big smiles and purposed
to go back later for more. Jack and I would slip into the
office, one at a time, over the next few days sipping from
the crystal decanter while the other one would stand
guard outside the door in the main hall of the school.

The problem we soon faced was that our little well of
Burgundy was rapidly running dry! And we also faced
the inevitable – our crime would be found out! Two
schoolboys, when posed with such a problem, came up
with the perfect solution. We would pour water into the
decanter and drop some colouring crystals, stolen from

the science laboratory, into the water. It actually worked! I never heard a word about the water that was miraculously turned into Burgundy!

Once you get a taste for drugs, and particularly alcohol, you get this deep hunger to feed the habit. This normally leads to heartache, because sooner or later you have to cross the line of what is right to get what you desperately need. Jack and I faced another problem – our Burgundy supply was no longer available and we both wanted a drink. Jack had recently been in the headmaster's private living quarters, situated on the second floor of the main house, for a caning. While the cane was coming down across his bottom he was gazing straight at a fabulous drinks cabinet. The sight of all those bottles helped ease the pain of the thrashing, and the seeds of temptation were sown.

Sooner or later you have to cross the line of what is right to get what you desperately need

Somehow, we had to get access to the headmaster's quarters while he was out of the way. Now, every Tuesday morning the headmaster and his wife would treat themselves to a shopping trip for about half a day in Yeovil – that would be the time to get to the drinks cabinet without being caught. The plan came together quickly, as we realised that the school sick bay was part of the headmaster's quarters. The sick bay was, in fact, only a small room with a large window looking out onto an internal yard in the school complex. The room boasted two beds, with little else. The best yet was that the only access was down a little flight of steps through the headmaster's hallway inside his quarters. That was it, we would somehow get into the sick bay and wait for the couple to go out shopping in Yeovil.

Monday morning came and, feeling nervous after the morning break, I went to find matron in her office on the ground floor. Stepping into her office and trying to look convincing as someone who had just vomited, I complained of being sick. I couldn't believe it – it actually worked. This hardened matron took one look at me and marched me up to see the headmaster's wife. She was a hard one to crack. After many questions and taking my temperature she finally allowed me access to the sick bay. Lying in the fresh linen and enjoying the escape from a boring history lesson, I smiled to myself, knowing that the first part of the mission was accomplished and successful. During Monday night, there was a disturbance at the headmaster's door. Jack, in his pyjamas, was almost crying to the headmaster that he had been sick in one of the toilets and wanted to have something for it. The headmaster, who was hopeless in such matters, called for his wife. She finally came, moaning about the late hour and this time said that maybe it was a bug going around the school. Jack was promptly placed in the sick bay, with a bowl by his bed. Then everyone went back to sleep. The next day was hard, as we both had to justify our being in the sick bay. We should have been nominated for an 'Oscar' for our performance, as it worked!

The headmaster's wife told us that if we needed anything we would have to go down the main staircase – that was normally strictly forbidden – and see the school secretary in her office for help.

It seemed to take an eternity for them to go, but finally they went. When we heard them go through the main doors we knew it was party time! What a time we had as we drank from the different bottles of wines and spirits, lying on the headmaster's bed and watching his colour television.

To have been caught would have meant expulsion that very day, and probably six of the best for good measure. The alcoholic cocktails we were swigging soon began to go to our heads and it was a miracle that we left the room for the sick bay when we did. Jack had some mints, which were hot, but we sucked them anyway in case the head-master's wife wanted to check our temperatures again and would get wind of the booze on our breath.

We sank into those sick bay beds and chalked up another victory against law and order, and against the headmaster and his wife. We could never repeat that Tuesday morning as they would never have bought the fact that the two boys, who were sick together last time, were sick together again. But we had done it, and the thrill of that, for now, was enough to carry us until we felt the need for the next escapade.

Crime

Every criminal likes to think they have a code of so-called honour! I guess up to that point I had not really stolen much from fellow schoolchildren, but that was all to change at the school as I stretched myself to new limits of shame. When I first enrolled they sent a list of things to bring as a boarder. One such thing was a tuck box, something I had never heard of before. In reality, all it consisted of was a box, strengthened by metal corners and a lid fitted with a padlock for security. Everyone had a tuck box in which they could store valuables such as cameras, cash, jewellery, radios, etc. and also sweets and other edible luxuries. Tuck boxes on the whole meant 'Stay away from my property!' but to the criminal they were a piece of cake to open in such a way that nobody would know until it was too late.

Jack and I were good mates and, not only did we steal the headmaster's drink but we collaborated together to steal from the students as well. I soon lost all my scruples when I knew that these children had very wealthy parents or sponsors. We would particularly go for the Arab students' tuck boxes, as they would normally have lots of money, drink, cigarettes and dirty magazines. Once they had discovered that they had been robbed they were helpless: after all, how can you report stolen what was forbidden in the first place!

Saturday nights were a good time for a hit on the tuck boxes, as most of the older Arabs had been to Yeovil and stocked up well with forbidden pleasures. While they watched videos in their common room, Jack and I would steal down into the cellar corridor. This was, in fact, an old wine cellar, complete with all the old stone shelves. The tuck boxes were normally placed one on each shelf and within easy reach for anyone to get access to them. One of us would keep guard at the end of the cellar, while the other, armed with a screwdriver, would undo the hinges of the lid at the back of the tuck box. It was a fiddly job and difficult while your heart pounded wildly with the fear of being caught. But, as the old motto of the SAS goes, 'Who Dares Wins', and a rich booty, indeed, was found in those tuck boxes.

As the old motto of the SAS goes, 'Who Dares Wins'

Jack and I would be set up for the week, with a bountiful supply of cigarettes. Once the dirty deed had been done, we would go for a walk around the school fields, smoking and swigging Scotch or vodka straight from a bottle stolen from one of our Arab friends. Thankfully, we were never caught, for to be caught would have meant a good kicking from the victims and probably immediate expulsion from the school.

Pornography

It's probably a boy thing, but almost every boy growing up loves to look at the lurid, glossy photos of a pornographic magazine. The pages filled with the exposed flesh of models, some old enough to be their mums, hold an attraction to many lads reaching puberty. I, like many others, found pictures of naked women fascinating. I had seen younger girls with no clothes on, but the women in the pictures were much more interesting. I would gaze upon the images for hours and read the stories of erotica, gasping at the so-called sexual adventures of some men. I learned later in life that sex within marriage is undefiled and part of God's plan for a married couple. In fact, sex is a wonderful wedding gift from heaven for those who are married, but it's only intended for the wedding night onwards! I didn't know that at the time, and so wanted all the sex I could get.

One Saturday morning, as the rain came down, as it often did in that picturesque Somerset hamlet, an older friend asked me if I wanted to see a video. Out of boredom and sensing the excitement in the older lad, I said yes. I followed him and another lad into the video room. The video room was not far from the woodwork room. It had rising staging, so a capacity crowd could squeeze in and watch educational films during geography lessons. Well this film was a real 'education'! It had been borrowed from one of the Arab boys and was red hot! As the images began to appear on the screen I thought it was a medical film, because of the explicit close-up shots of the human genitalia. It was only when the sound was turned up and I heard the ecstatic moans of the women being filmed that I realised I was watching my first hard-core porno film. As I watched the screen in that dark room, I found the images strangely compelling, although I knew that it wasn't right to observe such things in a voyeuristic way.

Those guilty feelings soon dissipated as I grew older, and pornography had a strong hold on my teenage emotions. Because of pornography, I viewed women as sexual objects of desire. Pornography twisted my own sexuality from what was a normal sex drive in a teenager, to a depraved lusting for sexual conquest. It cheapened women in my understanding, defiling my heart with its dark and dangerous passions that in some men lead to serious crimes against women.

Fire and Lies

One of the most serious crimes a person can commit is arson. Starting fires can lead to devastation and loss of life and carries with it heavy penalties. Monday afternoons saw us lining up outside Mr Mason's classroom for geography lessons. Normally it was boring stuff, like rock formation and the course of rivers, but today it was going to be good, as he had promised us an orienteering field trip in a plantation some miles from the school. The minibus was full of excited kids, keen to be out of the classroom for a bit of fun, even if it was only for the afternoon. Once parked up at the plantation, we were told to split up into pairs and to get on with our map reading exercises.

Mark and I set off together to do our assigned tasks. Once out of the sight of everyone else, Mark pulled up his trouser

leg to reveal this fabulous diving knife in a holster strapped
to his ankle. I was well impressed as he reached for it and
handed it to me. With the sun gleaming on the blade, I
wished I had a knife like that. Mark explained that it was
pretty good as a throwing knife, and he showed me its flight
power as he aimed at a plantation tree. The throw was excellent; the problem was Mark's poor sense of direction, as the
knife sped past the tree at supersonic speed and landed in
the deep grass behind. Mark was devastated, as he had 'borrowed' it from his dad without asking and now it was lost.
We searched for it in the deep grass that was yellow and dry
due to the summer's drought. After about ten minutes, and
with Mark still despairing, I had a brainwave: we should set
fire to the grass and then when it was burned we would find
the knife. Mark actually had some matches with him and so
in seconds we had set fire to the small area where we had
been desperately searching. That was a big mistake! One
match ignited that grass instantly and within moments a
mighty inferno blazed before us,
with flames soaring above us far too
large to stomp out with our feet. In
a panic, we ran away and stopped
to catch our breath. We knew that if
Within moments
a mighty inferno
blazed before us
we were caught, this would place
us both in the most serious trouble.
The little patch we had lit had now
become very large, with the flames
leaping from tree to tree. There was
only one thing for it, we would run and find Mr Mason and
tell him we had discovered a fire. Once alerted, he told us to
shout for all the other children and gather together while he
alerted the ranger and the fire service.

By the time the first fire engine came into the plantation, many acres, valued at thousands of pounds, had

been totally destroyed. All the class helped to fight the blaze: taking off our school jumpers we beat the flames out. Finally it was under control, and as we walked back to the minibus the firemen hailed us as young heroes! Once we returned to the school, I had the cheek to campaign to Mr Mason on behalf of the class that we might seek compensation for our damaged shoes and clothes!

There were suspicions, though, and the police came to speak to the headmaster and Mr Mason. We were not interviewed directly by the police, probably because of our young age, but we all had to make written statements in our own handwriting of the events of that Monday afternoon field trip. Mark and I had conspired already to say the same thing and so we got away with what could have been fatal to everyone walking in the plantation that Monday afternoon.

There is so much more I could write about my days at the school. I had grown up quickly: from the age of 11 to 13 I had been on a fast track of discovery. I had now clearly left the innocence of childhood behind, and with a heart that was cold and hard, I faced the world and all it would throw at me. I stole, swore, drank alcohol, smoked, took drugs, slept with girls, loved pornography and practised the dark arts of the occult. The school had certainly been an experience. In fact, for me it was like entering through the gateway into the kingdom of darkness: a kingdom of evil that had taken me captive and would

> *My whole life was taken over by dark satanic forces. Dark forces that would eventually try to destroy me and take my very life*

never want to let me go until my whole life was taken over by dark satanic forces. Dark forces that would eventually try to destroy me and take my very life.

6

GO TO JAIL

I had decided to leave the Somerset boarding school. After spending almost two years there, I had finally had enough of the regime. The social services arranged for me to stay permanently at the children's home. They also secured a place for me at a local secondary school. It was an all boys' school right in the centre of Poole, beside the bus station. The old building was in a poor state of repair and the constant exhaust fumes of heavy traffic had blackened the red brick walls.

It was during the days of the summer holiday before I was due to start at my new school that I had been charged and summoned to appear, at a later date, before Poole Juvenile Court. During the lunch break on my first day at the school, Mrs Clark, my class teacher, asked to see me. She was a lady in her sixties and reminded me of Dame Edna Everage. Although she was a strict lady and had high standards when it came to manners and work performance, she was also kind. She explained to me that she knew all about my upcoming court appearance, and reassured me that if I behaved myself in her lessons she would give a good report of me to the court.

The days seemed to go quickly at secondary school. I wasn't that happy there, but then I probably wasn't going to be happy at any school. I enjoyed my art lessons and would take great satisfaction in painting watercolours. The art room was upstairs, above some storerooms, right by the side of Poole bus station. The art teacher was a strange sort of man who seemed to be a magnet for all the other teachers. They would come up to his small class office and drink tea with him, discussing all their problems, I guess. There was never a lesson when he didn't have a visitor to entertain. We just got on with whatever we wanted to do. Some painted, some carved objects out of lumps of white plaster, some just sat and read, while others would sit in the corner and tattoo themselves with the India ink and needles! When we had an art lesson we were never allowed to go upstairs to the room until the teacher came down to get us. Come rain or shine we always had to wait!

It was while waiting outside the art room that I had my first fight at the school. Every class has its bullies and troublemakers and there were a few in mine! There were three lads who all came from the same neighbourhood and they seemed to be on a mission to make the rest of the class miserable. They would punch and kick other lads and steal their lunch money and cigarettes if they had any. Not a single day would go by without them ganging up on someone.

One particular day, they decided to pick on me outside the art room.

> *I put my school bag and coat down and began to put my fists up. That was it! The class became like a pack of bloodhounds baying for action*

One of the terrible three was the big mouth. He would usually wind people up and, once someone retaliated in self-defence, the other two would come muscling in. This lad started accusing me of something or other and I wasn't having it. He then began to push me around, hoping for a response. He sure got one, as I put my school bag and coat down and began to put my fists up. That was it! The class became like a pack of bloodhounds baying for action.

There was no question of my stepping down, I had the honour of my name to defend now. Within seconds we were grappling with each other. I felt a sharp pain in my leg as one of the other bullies kicked me for good measure. I knew I had to carry on and so forgot about the other two and went for the first lad with all I had. I landed a full fist straight into his nose, instantly bringing him blood and pain. His guard was down and so I continued to punch his face as hard as I could. The other bullies realised they had got more than they had bargained for, but out of loyalty to their friend they dragged me off him just as the art teacher appeared. That was a close call! From that time on, I was never bullied by those three lads again, for I had won their respect and the admiration of the other lads.

Maths was one subject I loathed. I was hopeless with fractions and division, along with the other lads in my class, and so the maths teacher despaired of us! He was from Liverpool and football mad. He often told us that we would never be any good at maths, so we might as well all go out and play football! And we did, running and shouting on the sports pitch during maths lessons to the envy of all the other classes. The days it rained we would go over to the public library and spend our time in the reference section. Sitting in the library during maths lessons was fun, but I did have a feeling of being cheated. After all, the maths teacher was head of year and should have made a determined effort to get us enjoying our sums and being confident to enter the adult world with at least an elementary understanding of arithmetic.

One day, as we went into the classroom, we found him with his face in his hands doubled over his desk openly crying. It was the day millions around the world wept, as the news reports came through that John Lennon had been murdered. The teacher was a Liverpudlian in his forties, and the Beatles were everything to him. Now someone had shot down one of his heroes on a New York street. We never did any maths that day, as our teacher gave us a history lesson on the world-renowned 'Fab Four' instead.

Special Fostering

One day, Auntie Jenny, the officer in charge at the children's home, called me into her office and chatted to me about special fostering. I had already told my social worker that I felt that I needed to be out of the children's home after the Juvenile Court incident and, knowing how I was feeling, the social services decided to place me in a special foster home. This 'new breed' of carers did it professionally and were paid for their services! My social worker took me one evening to a home not too far away from the children's home. The couple, Brian and Jane, together with their son and daughter welcomed me that night. They went overboard in making me feel at home and before I knew it I was agreeing to leave the children's home to live with them. It only took a few weeks to organise my new residence, which was strange for the bureaucracy of the social services!

On the first night in my new home, I couldn't help wondering if I had made a bad mistake! Jane had cooked tea for everybody, but because I was late home I had to sit in the dining room and eat on my own. I enjoyed my meal and once I had finished, I rose and went to the sink to wash up my plate and cutlery. A simple task done, I went to go upstairs to my room, when all of a sudden Jane came out of the lounge, where she had been sitting quietly with the others and inspected the kitchen. In doing the washing up I had left a few soap bubbles on the draining board. That was it! All hell broke loose as she ranted at me about keeping the house tidy. The noise brought Brian into the kitchen and to be fair he defended me as a 16-year-old boy who had at least appreciated the meal and had made the effort to wash up. Startled by the response of Jane, I went to my room and stayed out of sight for the rest of the evening. I knew then that I wasn't going to get on with Jane. She was a lady who suffered a great deal of pain with her back, and because of these spinal problems she was very irritable with almost everyone in the house throughout the day. I don't mind people having a shout – after all, as the television advert says, 'Its good to talk!' I could put up with a good portion of 'tongue pie' from Jane, but those long periods of sulky, heavy and resentful atmospheres were awful.

They wondered why I never wanted to be with them. They asked why I never ate with them, why I didn't want to go shopping with them and so on. It was because of Jane. I learned to hate her and, when she used to scream out verbal abuse at me, I'd wish she would drop dead. Brian would try to pacify her, but it was no use. If I watched the television with them and got up to use the toilet, she would pull herself out of her chair in pain and reshuffle the cushions on the couch, even though she knew I would be returning shortly!

> *When she used to scream out verbal abuse at me, I'd wish she would drop dead*

The special foster home was supposed to support me, to care for me and give me the confidence I needed as I was entering young adulthood. Living with this family was absolute misery for me, and so I stayed out late from the home, filling my evenings with casual sex, drinking and committing crimes.

School was rapidly coming to an end, and as part of a national initiative we were all offered 'Work Experience'. As I scanned down the list of local tradesmen who were willing to have a schoolchild for a week's experience of their particular trade, my eyes fell upon 'Dewhurst the Master Butchers'. I knew as soon as I saw the word 'Butchers' that it was for me. Once I had applied, the wheels were set in motion and I found myself reporting to Mr Clay, the shop manager, early one Monday morning.

The smell of a butcher's shop is unique – a sweet aroma of flesh and blood mixed with the distinct smell of sawdust that always covered the tiled floor. The butchers were all reasonably young, and as I could make a good brew of tea I fitted in instantly. They taught me how to present the pies in the chilled cabinet, how to slice ham and corned beef so thin that you could read the paper through it. I learned how to sharpen the big steak knives with a butcher's steel and how to grind a boning knife blade so sharp it would split a hair. This was far better than being in school!

The hours were long and I got no pay, but the reward of job satisfaction was immense. Every day I grasped some new angle of this traditional man's trade, from cutting the carcasses down to making burgers and sausages. I felt so proud when I stood dressed in a pristine pressed white butcher's coat with a striped apron and sporting a butcher's boater hat. There I was behind the counter, actually serving the great British public.

Mr Clay was pretty strict, but we got on very well, as I was always keen to learn and better myself. The others were a wealth of information, not of the meat kind, but on wine, women and song! I would stand there listening for ages as they told me all sorts of things about life that I had never heard before. My work experience soon came to an end, but because I had excelled in the short time I was there, the district manager promised me a job at the Poole shop as soon as I left school! That was something to be proud of because, out of a class of thirty, I was the only lad who left school with a good job to go to. I really didn't care about my forthcoming exams any more, not once I knew I was going to be a butcher earning £63.00 a week!

I left school and started at Dewhurst the Butchers, in Poole High Street, as a full-time trainee butcher. I continued to impress the district manager so much that he enrolled me on a college course every Wednesday at Bournemouth, for the Institute of Meat. I enjoyed the course and passed my exams. I loved the job. I enjoyed all the other aspects of my life, but I still wasn't happy. Deep down, I was empty. How that was possible, I didn't know then. After all, my days were full of activities – some legitimate, some illegitimate. But as a friend of mine once said, 'You can have a full life, but without Jesus, it's not life to the full!'[4]

'You can have a full life, but without Jesus, it's not life to the full!'

Poole Speedway

Although I was working, I kept in contact with Colin and Shane, who were both still at the children's home. Most evenings we would be up to trouble of one sort or another. I certainly preferred their company to Brian and Jane's! I'm not sure who had the original idea, but we decided together one night to go to the speedway stadium and try our luck on the clubhouse and bar attached to the racetrack.

So as not to arouse Brian and Jane's suspicions, I went to bed as normal that night, setting my alarm clock for 2 a.m. When the alarm went off, just a few hours later, I quietly rose from my bed, got dressed in dark clothes and put a pair of black leather gloves and a torch in my jacket pocket. I reached under the bed for my claw hammer and stuck it in my belt. Then, holding my breath, I eased the window open and climbed out onto the porch roof. Closing the window almost shut, I jumped to the ground. The soft front lawn broke my fall and I landed with a gentle thud. Then it was a brisk walk to meet Colin and Shane in the car park of the speedway stadium. Walking along the quiet road into Poole town centre, I lit up a cigarette and couldn't help thinking, with crooked pride, that I was such a professional thief!

Once at the car park, we made our plan. We would climb over a wall and drop down into the track area of the stadium. From there, we would break an entry into the bar area via the toilet blocks that joined the spectator area to the club and bar complex. Like commandos blacked out for covert action, we set our plan into motion. Seconds later and out of breath, we were hiding in the shadows of the spectator seats. The external door to the toilets would somehow have to be opened if our plans were to go any further. Using the hammer and a screwdriver that Shane had brought, we soon crudely chiselled away enough wood to jemmy open the lock with the claw of the hammer. With the sound of splintering wood and then a crack as the door flew open under force, we were in!

The corridor led to the toilet block. We had to get into the toilets to reach our objective – the bar that we hoped would be filled with cash, cigarettes and bottles of spirits. We were one door down and two more to go. The second door was easy: I sat on the floor of the corridor, back against the wall and both feet at the bottom of the door. As I applied the pressure of all my bodyweight against the poorly-manufactured internal door, it gave way almost instantly. My brute force had made a large cat flap and we were through. In the toilets we realised that the next internal door could well be alarmed. With this in mind, we chiselled the lock away using the screwdriver and hammer as before. Once the carpentry was over, we were ready. It was going to be a quick hit: every man for himself, grabbing what he could and getting out before the alarm attracted the attention of the police.

I gave the door a powerful kick and it flew open immediately. Dashing to the bar, we began to grab what we could. To our disgust and disappointment the cash till was empty, the drawer open, but no money to be found. I turned instead to the shelves filled with all the different packets of cigarettes. Taking a carrier bag from my pocket I literally filled it to the top with cigarettes. At least I had got something, but now the fear of being caught made me want to get out of the place as fast as I could.

Running for the toilet door, I noticed the headlights of a car approaching the club from the front car park. I knew it – they had a silent alarm! The others saw the lights as well, and followed me as we dashed through the broken doors and leapt out into the starry night again, fleeing the scene as we ran across the speedway track and over the far side boundary fence.

My heart beating wildly, I ran down the walkway running along the main railway line into Poole station. We crouched in the darkness by the footbridge and quickly divided the spoil. Not much, just about twenty packets of cigarettes each and a few quart bottles of vodka and Scotch. We agreed to split up and meet the next night, and with that, we slipped away separately into the shadows of the coming dawn.

I was able to sell the stolen goods quickly to the guys with whom I was working. They were happy with cut-price cigarettes and booze, so I gained a little money from my night job!

Although the cash incentive wasn't much, the idea of hitting the speedway stadium a second time did appeal to me. I needed the buzz that only a criminal knows as he commits a crime; the excitement and rush of adrenaline as I entered into the arena of dishonesty. The kicks I got out of burglary and other crimes gave me a fix that, although temporary, somehow eased the inner pain and emptiness of my life.

Later, as I explained my plans to Colin and Shane, they found the prospect of a second hit just as exciting as I did – after all, the stadium probably hadn't fixed the doors yet, and they really wouldn't expect burglars to strike twice in two days, surely? We executed our plan exactly as we had the night before. The outer door hadn't been fixed properly: it was just held shut with a piece of wood screwed as a crude latch. Inside, the only door repaired was the third door leading directly into the bar. Again, no money, but the cigarettes had been restocked, so we filled our bags again and grabbed a few quart bottles of spirits for good measure and then, once again, we stole away into the night.

The next day I met with Shane. Colin was unable to meet us, so we had a McDonald's and talked about what

crime we would embark on that night. Shane asked
whether I had seen the massive Scotch bottle on the side
of the bar with coins and five-pound notes in. The bottle
was being filled for some charity, and now Shane was
suggesting we go back and steal it. The idea seemed
good. We wouldn't have to split the proceeds three ways,
but two, as Colin wasn't with us. I had a gut feeling that
something bad might happen, but Shane kept saying,
'Third time lucky!'

I was feeling tired after the other two nights of breaking
and entering, so this time I got out of the house quietly and
walked to the nearest telephone box. In those days, you
would still find a dirty, foul-smelling directory sitting on the
shelf. Looking up a taxi firm, I called one out and waited for
the car to pick me up. The taxi arrived and, stupidly, I asked
the driver to drop me off at the stad-
ium. The driver, on being paid,
drove off. I was early now, but,
lighting up a cigarette, I walked
over to the dark shadows of the car
park and waited. After what
seemed ages, a figure appeared out
of the darkness – Shane – smiling
and ready for action.

*Tyres screeched to a
halt just outside the
front of the club. I
could see the flash-
ing blue lights of
the police cars*

Once again, we vaulted over the fence and made our
way through the three doors that led to our little Aladdin's
cave. Dashing into the bar for the third time, I knew then,
deep down inside, that this was not going to be a lucky
hit! Just as I picked up the bottle, which was incredibly
heavy, tyres screeched to a halt just outside the front of the
club. I could see the flashing blue lights of the police cars,
and I realised that now was a good time to get out, quick!

Refusing to give up the bottle filled with cash, I picked
it up and we both ran, as before, over the speedway track

to the far side of the stadium. Running along the footpath to make our escape from the now pursuing police officers, we approached the footbridge, and I was horrified to see policemen running towards us – we were trapped! With nothing to lose, I ran at one of the officers, who tackled me to the floor. As I went flying, the bottle fell from my arms and smashed onto the tarmac, sending almost two hundred pounds worth of change in every direction. The policemen were furious, as they had to pick up every penny. Later it would be used as evidence against us!

The arresting officers cautioned us immediately and then forcefully marched us over the footbridge to a waiting police transit van on the main road. Sitting inside the police van, a feeling of sickness came upon me as we drove through the dark streets of Poole to the police station.

I had been in trouble before, but now I knew this was the big time; this time it was going to be tough. After I had been presented to the charge sergeant and all my personal effects had been stripped from me and signed for, I was led to an empty cell. Sleep refused to come, although I tried to lie down on the thin mattress and shut my eyes. I just couldn't rest, as thoughts of what would happen next flooded my mind, and I was swamped in anxiety. I tried to shout out through the cell door to Shane, but he was on the other side of the prisoners' exercise yard and couldn't hear me. Somehow, I needed to communicate with him, so that our story would hold up under the experienced scrutiny of the CID investigating officers, who would certainly be interrogating us in the morning.

With the daylight came breakfast, and then the CID. The plain-clothes officers had a whole book of petty crimes to throw at someone and they chose me as their fall guy. Basically, if I admitted to petty burglaries, etc., they would present them to the court as crimes 'to be taken into consideration'. If I co-operated with the police, normally such crimes would go unpunished. The police would come out as heroes – their crime clear-up rate would be up! They spent all day trying to pin crimes on me that I knew I had never committed. However, some of the scenes of crime they described were my handiwork, but I wasn't going to tell them that!

We had been caught red-handed and so had to expect to be charged with that crime. And, although we denied the first two burglaries at the stadium, they weren't buying it, as it was obvious that the same gang had worked each night. I was marched down to the charge sergeant and, in the presence of a social worker, officially charged with burglary.

Custody

Later that day, I stood with Shane in the dock of Poole Magistrates' Court. The hearing lasted only a few minutes, but the outcome wasn't good. The chairman of the magistrates ordered that we both be remanded in custody until the next week, as reports would have to be compiled on us.

There were so many prisoners to be taken to the prison that day, that an official police van for transporting prisoners was ordered. The cons called this mode of transport 'the horse box' because the van was split up into little cells designed for about two men each. In reality, four prisoners were crammed in for the ride from the courthouse to Dorchester prison.

The journey to Dorchester consisted of listening to a young man who had already been remanded at Dorchester prison. He took it upon himself to tell us what to expect once we arrived. He warned us about the violence and the homosexuals, who would pounce on younger men in the showers, viciously raping them.

Once the great gates of Dorchester prison had shut on us, we were taken from the custody van and herded like cattle up a ramp and into the prison induction wing. I realised then that this was going to be no picnic! We were told to sit on a bench while the paperwork was completed. Once the induction officer was satisfied that the police had brought the right number of prisoners, he signed for us, and the police left: their job done.

This was going to be no picnic!

When my name was called, I went through into another room with a desk, at which sat two prison officers, whom we all referred to as 'screws'. I was ordered to strip off and so, in red-faced humiliation, I began to remove my clothing hoping that when I had got down to my pants, they would say 'stop', but they didn't! Standing completely naked in front of them, I was further humiliated as they asked me various questions, while other prisoners and officers walked back and forth. Then one of the screws left the desk and stood next to me. He asked me to open my mouth for him, and after that ordered me to touch my toes so that he could check that I had not concealed any drugs about my person. Finally, he allowed me to straighten up and told me to go for the 'sheep dip', which was the obligatory bath for every prisoner inducted into the prison system.

Once bathed, I was thrown a set of prison clothes, complete with the striped 'Ronnie Barker' shirt of *Porridge* fame. The clothes were far too big and I had a job to hold up my trousers. I had other things on my mind at that point, which were far more important. Where were the homosexuals who were waiting to rape me? When could I have a smoke?

I was placed in a small holding cell with two other youths and a couple of older men. We talked about our crimes and were speculating about our possible sentences when the door flew open and tea was served! We each had a stainless steel tray with three compartments on it; a large one for the main dish, some sort of stew and mashed potato, and the others for bread and a type of sponge and custard pudding. The cell went quiet for a moment, then, one by one we complained about the food. One of the older men, a seasoned con, told us we were lucky, as the food was particularly good that day!

Sometime later, the door opened again and we were being led into the main prison and up the stairs to the Youth Wing on the second floor. The taunts and shouts of abuse flew from some of the hardened men behind the locked doors. Tobacco was offered as payment if we would prostitute ourselves, and others mocked us calling us 'Baby Burglars'. Eventually, the great barred gate and the secondary locked door of the Youth Wing were opened, and the officer shouted out, 'Two on, Sir.' An officer appeared from the wing office. He was wearing a white shirt, which I soon discovered meant he was a senior officer. He ordered us into his office and then went through the regime of the Youth Wing.

It was all pretty straightforward really. Wake up, wash, breakfast. Locked in your cell until lunchtime, out to collect your lunch and then back in the cell until teatime. Out to collect your tea, then, if you're lucky, you get one hour of association time, which basically means watching the telly on the landing, and then it's bedtime! We were supposed to get daily exercise, but that would depend upon the weather! As there were neither coats nor umbrellas, if it was raining, all we could do was to look longingly out through the bars and hope for better weather the next day.

Although I hated every moment of languishing in the Youth Wing of Dorchester prison, it had one good point – I wouldn't have to go on holiday with Brian and Jane. They had been making me save to pay for my own air-fare to go with them all for a family holiday on the Costa Brava. All I knew, as Jane held out her hand each week, was that it 'Costa Lot'! I was dreading those hours that would be spent on the beach with Jane moaning at everything and Brian trying to keep the peace. I don't think I hated many people, but in the short time I lived with that family I learned to hate them. Such were my feelings toward them that prison was a luxury holiday, compared to the hell they would have made the Costa Brava!

Brian came to see me a few times – I felt, more out of obligation than care. When he came he only moaned at me and told me what a fool I was in missing the 'won-derful holiday'. To be fair, Brian at least made an effort, but Jane had given up on me and, as I had no time for her, I really didn't care.

Dorchester was a typical Victorian prison, complete with its own hanging shed and graveyard! The Youth Wing, along with the rest of the prison, was severely over-crowded. Three men occupied cells designed to incarcer-ate one prisoner. Each cell had a bunk bed and a single bed. This meant there was no room to move. In fact the area your bed took up was your personal space. You could spend all day sitting on your bed, as there was lit-erally nowhere else to go. To walk, under escort, down the stairs three times a day to fetch your meals, was the height of luxury and the full extent of a day's exercise if it was raining!

There was a toilet block at the end of the wing, consisting of two toilets without any doors for privacy, a urinal and one shower, again, with no door. There was also a big sink area with taps that was used to slop out human waste. The cells, being Victorian, had no toilet facilities, and during long times of 'bang up' such as night-time, when only a skeleton team of officers would be on duty, you would never be allowed out of the cell. This meant that you had to use the toilet pot that every prisoner is issued with at induction. To stand and urinate into a pot in the close confines of a small prison cell and have to do that in front of two other men is humiliating. However, it's part of prison life and you have to get used to it pretty quickly. Every morning, the stench of toilet pots being emptied of urine was foul. If you were lucky and were unlocked first, your first priority would be to get to the wash area before it was reduced to a sewerage works.

Every day was the same, boring lock-up, hour after hour after hour, with no let-up. Sometimes the boredom would be violently broken by the shrill sound of the prison emergency bell. The bell would be sounded if a fight had broken out and men needed to be separated. Once the bell sounded, no matter where you were – in the lunch queue or dripping wet in the shower – every prisoner was quickly locked into their cell until the situation was dealt with. I had heard about riots in the prison and was always glad to be locked away when the emergency bell sounded, as you could not be sure of your personal safety if you were out of your cell when the bell rang.

Every wing in prison has its drug and tobacco barons. These are the convicts that spend their time lending tobacco and drugs to other prisoners, but at an astronomical rate of interest. To ensure they get their interest, they normally 'employ' a couple of heavies to collect the goods owed. The heavies would think nothing of using extreme violence to guarantee the baron receiving what was owed to him. During my prison experience, I would see lots of violence exacted on those foolish enough to borrow without having the ability to pay back. The prison system was hard and cruel, with many victims falling to 'unexplained' cuts and bruises inside. The weak were picked upon and 'taxed' for protection. When asked if you would like to be protected, if you said no, as you could look after yourself, you could well soon be nursing a bleeding nose! The experienced thugs of the prison regime knew when to strike: normally, just as the screws were doing something else and so would miss any violence.

Some men just couldn't stand the bullying and the fear of being attacked by other prisoners, so they opted for Rule 43. Rule 43 is when a prisoner applies to the Governor to be locked away in segregation from the main prison body for his own protection. Sometimes, if a thug or baron was caught bullying, he would be removed from the wing to protect the rest of the prisoners. Violence was very much a part of the day-to-day life of the prison, and many times I found myself worrying about death threats because I refused to give my tobacco – or 'burn' as it's commonly referred to by the cons – to one of the prison bullies. One man, who shared my cell, was taken into the wash area and shaved literally all over and then punched and kicked. His crime? He confessed to being a homosexual!

> *Violence was very much a part of the day-to-day life of the prison, and many times I found myself worrying about death threats*

The Youth Wing had a six-man cell. This was very unusual in my prison experience, but considered a luxury because there were more windows and more floor space to move around the bunk beds. Once the lights went out at night-time talking was forbidden, but sleep often eluded us, as the bright orange glow of the security lights flooded through the cell windows. I cannot remember one night of darkness during the whole of my time in prison! Although talking was banned, we talked for hours. We planned new crimes, plotted how to rob banks and shared memories of passionate nights with the women in our lives. We would talk into the next day! It would help us escape the harsh reality that liberty had been stripped from us, and give us hope that one day we would be free once again.

One evening we decided that we would hold a séance in our cell, once the lights had gone out. To do this we stole a glass from the wing classroom while we had cleaning duties. We also wrote out all the letters of the alphabet and numbers from zero to nine. In addition to this, we wrote 'yes' and 'no' on two other pieces of paper.

That night, when the lights had been turned off, we leapt from our beds and pulled a cupboard, with a flat Formica top, away from the cell wall. Assembling all the pieces of paper on the flat surface of the cupboard in the form of a Ouija board, I organised the séance. Placing the glass in the middle of the board, I instructed all the men to place one finger each upon the glass. We all began to concentrate quietly, focusing upon the spirit world. Suddenly the glass began to move slowly around the Ouija board. I began to question the spirit and the glass began to spell out the answers. The spirit told us that he had once been a prisoner at Dorchester and that he had committed suicide because he had been very unhappy. The whole séance was becoming depressive and, as the glass spelled out different answers, I got bored and asked the spirit if he could predict the future. On getting the answer 'Yes', I asked the spirit if one of us would die before we reached thirty. It answered 'Yes', and so I then asked how that person would die. The glass went to C...A...N... I said cancer and the glass violently sped to 'Yes' on the board. Foolishly, I asked the fateful question: which one of us would it be? The glass went flying over the surface of the board to one of the men called Stewart and tipped over. The guy nearly died there and then! But before he could, we heard the night screw come onto the landing. We had seconds to get into bed. Hiding the glass in the cupboard and shutting the door, also putting all the pieces of lettered paper in the drawer, we just made it, as the prison officer opened up the security flap and gazed into our cell. Once his footsteps faded into the night we wiped the sweat from our brows, but then something happened that shook us all.

As we heard the clock tower in the centre of Dorchester strike midnight, suddenly the cupboard door flew open with a crash and before our eyes, the glass we had hidden floated out from the back of the cupboard, violently smashing on the floor just where Stewart had been standing! If that wasn't frightening enough, the drawer slid open of its own accord and all the lettered pieces of paper we had used for our Ouija board blew out, slowly floating to the floor like large confetti. One of the men almost wet himself with sheer horror and began to recite the Lord's Prayer.

> *As we heard the clock tower in the centre of Dorchester strike midnight, suddenly the cupboard door flew open with a crash*

The next day, two of the men asked to be transferred to another cell – they were too frightened to stay with us any

longer. I knew that the kingdom of darkness was for real,
but things that went bump in the night didn't scare me!

Crown Court

The days on remand soon came to an end, and before I
knew it, Shane and I were on our way under escort to
Bournemouth Crown Court. Once we had been placed in
the cellblock deep under the court, drinks were made and
we had a brief visit from our solicitors and the defending
barristers. We were told that a custodial sentence was very
probable, but it would not be too long, due to the fact that
we had already been in custody for about four months.

Our names were called and we were led up two flights
of steps to a landing just below the dock. At the given signal, we were told to ascend the final steep staircase leading to the infamous dock. The clerk stood and said, 'Court
rise.' We all stood as the judge came in. To our horror it
was the same man who had sat at Poole Juvenile Court
some years before! The charges were duly read, and we
had to stand and make our plea. Due to the fact that we
were caught red-handed, there was no point in pleading
'not guilty', so we pleaded 'guilty' and were told to sit
down again. After what seemed like ages, the judge
retired to consider his sentencing upon us.

When he returned I was asked to stand up. Heart beating wildly, I waited to hear him speak. He began to tell
me off, but finally summed up the sentence by ordering
me to do 150 hours of 'community service'.

The judge then told the court that he was being lenient
with me due to my troubled family life and the fact that I
had already served time as a prisoner remanded in
custody. He made it clear, however, that he was noting
the sentence, and if I should ever appear before his court

again he would have no choice but to give me the maximum sentence! I didn't care about his threat: after all, I would never see him again, or so I thought!

I skipped back down those steep steps to the cells rejoicing at my luck! As I signed for my personal belongings, my solicitor warned me in no uncertain terms that if I didn't conform to the community service order I would be back in court before my feet could touch the ground.

Brian came to fetch me and emphasised how lucky I was and that I should now be very careful who I hung around with, and all the other things I guess parents try to tell their kids at such times.

As we drove home from the court, I was dreading the reunion with Jane. Prison was awful, but living with her was hell! I wouldn't have to put up with her for long though, as I had decided that I would be moving out. Prison had changed me, and now I was going to do my own thing. The social services had had their say for too long: I was now going to make my own way in life. My heart was full of arrogance and pride: although I didn't realise it at the time, the Bible spoke about my condition saying, *'The human heart is most deceitful and desperately wicked.'*[5] That was me, and I was due for a big fall. Yes, the days ahead would take me into the final descent.

7

THE FINAL DESCENT

Liz was about 35 and I was 16, going on 17. She lived up the road from my real mum, and for some reason we just seemed to click. I had popped round one night to Mum's house with Colin and as we were drinking tea, a skinny woman came walking in without even knocking and made herself at home. Mum introduced this lady to me as a friend of hers from up the road, called Liz. I had been drinking earlier, and before long found myself flirting with this lady, who was almost old enough to be my mother. After Liz had gone I knew I wanted to see her again. My chance came the following week when John, Mum's husband, had some stolen goods to take up to Liz's house and asked me to do it, as he didn't feel well. More likely, he suspected that the police were watching the house and he didn't want to be caught red-handed with a load of 'hot' gear!

Liz came to the door and, by the smell of her breath, she had been on the bourbon, which was her favourite drink. When I entered the front room, I was amazed to see my Uncle Gary lying half drunk on the carpet. It turned out that Uncle Gary had just been released from Dorchester prison and was bringing a message to Liz from her husband Mark, who was doing a stretch for a drug-related crime. Uncle Gary obviously thought his luck was in that night, because he was chatting up Liz as if there were no tomorrow. I felt a challenge rising in me and, although I didn't think this 35-year-old woman would be interested in a 16-year-old boy, I decided to have a go anyway.

Uncle Gary didn't last long, as the drink began to get the better of him, and before long he was sprawled out, snoring on the floor. At this, Liz sat next to me and, within moments, we were kissing, and I found myself in the deep end with a married woman whose husband was in prison. I was excited at the time, as this woman was experienced and knew how to give a young man a good time. I felt neither guilt nor remorse that I was sleeping with another man's wife. I did realise that there would probably be a big fight when her husband was released from prison, but I kept that thought buried deep in my mind, while the power of sexual lust completely took me over. The sad thing is that today, many lose their personal purity through sexual immorality, in a bid to fill the emptiness of their lives. I had plenty of sex, but was I fulfilled? No! Happiness eluded me and the deep hunger in my heart for love was never satisfied by my sexual adventures.

One of the things I liked about Liz was that she had 'bottle'. She was fearless in her shoplifting escapades. John had a list of clients who would give their orders to him and then he'd tell Liz what was going to be needed. Liz would 'acquire' the goods and get a percentage of the article's retail value. She had a coat with dummy arms! It sounds crazy, but it worked well for her, as her hands would dart out of her coat and take expensive items, without anybody seeing what had taken place. I was amazed, as she would get hold of a Black and Decker hammer drill and conceal it under her coat in seconds.

Then she would go up to a security guard and ask where the light fittings were!

Before long, I was stealing the 'ordered goods' myself. Shoplifting to order with Liz was both exhilarating and dangerous, as she would often take risks that I wouldn't take. I think that because she had a little daughter, she believed that if she did get caught she wouldn't get a custodial sentence. Every time I walked into a shop with her I knew that I could have been caught. I considered myself to be pretty good, but pride comes before a fall, and I had a big fall coming!

I knew that I was trapped in a lifestyle with which I wasn't happy, but there seemed to be no other way of life open to me. My whole family were crooks, and all I was doing was following in their footsteps.

Drugs and alcohol were part of living. To survive, I needed these 'basics', along with sex and the thrill of crime, and Liz was the same. I had been happy with glue, and then different varieties of cannabis, but although I had every opportunity to buy LSD I never wanted to risk the experience of a 'bad trip'. So, I would get drunk on whisky instead, which for me was safe! Liz, on the other hand, had delved deeper into the misery of drugs, probably through her husband's influence, as he was a dealer. She would go out and buy some 'speed' and then inject herself, using syringes stolen from a local hospital just up the road.

The power of drug addiction is awful and stronger than many can understand. I remember one day when Liz was like a wildcat going crazy for a fix. She was abusive and looking ill, as she was drawn helplessly by the need of the next 'hit'. We drove into Bournemouth looking for the dealers with whom she would normally do business. After an hour of vain searching, Liz was getting desperate. Driving the car dangerously, she swerved up onto the pavement, near the centre of Bournemouth, leapt out of the car and ran after some-one walking into the crowd. Moments later, smiling, she jumped back into the car and drove near the sea front. Pulling up outside some men's toilets she jumped out of the car again, this time grabbing me with her. As we stood in the dirty cubical, she mixed the speed in a syringe and pulled down her jeans. In the squalor of that stinking toilet she jabbed the needle into a vein by her crotch. I knew then that I was smarter – this was not the answer to life. I had experienced some drugs, but knew this type of drug taking was not for me.

Driving the car dangerously, she swerved up onto the pavement

The relationship continued – it suited me fine at that young age. I did as I pleased during the day, working and stealing. Then during the evenings, I had as much sex as possible.

The great king of Israel called Solomon had all the money in the world. He had renowned fame and the most beautiful women in the world as his partners in bed. Yet, he was quoted as saying that it was all vanity. He had money, power and sex – the three things that most people are attracted to in the quest for life and satisfaction – yet he was empty. He had climbed to the top, and when he got there he was disillusioned by the view he saw.

He had money, power and sex – the three things that most people are attracted to in the quest for life and satisfaction

I, too, was disillusioned with life. I was doing just what I wanted and yet, through all the drugs, the crime and an active sex life, I was empty and miserable deep within. The hunger and desire for satisfaction needed to be fulfilled, and although I had a full life, in no way was I living life to the full.

Fright Night

My catalogue of crimes worsened by the day and, although I couldn't see it, I was now on a slippery downward spiral. During the day, I would work as a butcher, which I enjoyed, but almost every night I was breaking into a different property. Decency had become a word with which I was no longer familiar, as the crimes became more disgraceful.

One night, on my way to Liz's flat after working at the butcher's, I got a lift from Shane who, although he didn't possess a driving licence, was driving a car borrowed from a homosexual man who was attempting to groom Shane for sexual purposes. We passed by a large undertaker's firm and then I had a brainwave. We would break into this sinister place and see what we could steal. Shane wasn't too sure about it, as he was squeamish, but, being hardened by my experience as a butcher, I was adamant that it was a good idea. I believed that there would be money and also gold and diamond rings, which had been carefully put aside for the relatives of the deceased to collect later. I never once thought about the distress it would cause the grieving families, if they were to be informed that their loved ones' valuables had been stolen whilst in the safekeeping of the undertakers. After having some tea, I mentioned the idea to Liz, who was also squeamish. She said she wanted no part in it. So, after persuading Shane, we both went to the parlour late at night.

The street was busy with people returning home from the pubs, so we could afford the noise of breaking glass as the cars sped by the main road on which the funeral parlour was situated. We jumped over the main wall, ran across the turf and then leapt over the main gates into the complex. Hiding in the shadows, I waited beside a window which had a roller blind pulled down inside. Patiently, I bided my time, clothed in dark jeans and a black leather jacket with matching gloves. I held a hammer in my hand and, just as a large freight lorry from the port rolled past, I smashed the window.

Within seconds, we had climbed through the window, stepping onto broken glass. I penetrated the darkness of that room with the torch I pulled from inside my jacket. There in front of us were three empty slabs. Jackpot! We had got the right room first time. For some, this place would have been creepy, and Shane was beginning to get nervous. I kept reassuring him that dead people couldn't hurt him and that they wouldn't tell any tales either.

Along the side of the room was a long row of cupboards with a top filled with all sorts of surgical instruments of the funeral trade. In the corner was a coffin laid on trestles, lid screwed down and flowers resting on top, that looked creepy, but the best was to come. Along the other wall there were three great doors. I went to the nearest and pulled on the big handle which opened the door and revealed a large fridge. Like most household fridges, a light conveniently came on as the door opened, so I switched off my torch and gazed in.

What a sight! There in front of me were three dead people

What a sight! There in front of me were three dead people. I didn't look for too long, but the mental image of that stayed with me for some time. By now Shane had had enough!

However, I was only just beginning. A sense of macabre boldness had come upon me. I felt that as I had come this far, breaking new barriers of crime by violating the place of the dead, I may as well get as much as I possibly could. I pacified Shane by telling him to look for the keys to the hearse or one of the limousines, explaining we could go for a joyride! While Shane went off in one direction, I went into the hall of the funeral home, and to my surprise, found the office door unlocked.

This was all too easy, and it got better as I slipped into the funeral director's leather swivel chair behind the desk. The desk was locked, but using the claw of the hammer, I had it open very quickly. There was nothing inside the drawer but a leather pouch with a lock on it and it was open! Shining my torch beam onto the pouch in my hand I pulled out about three hundred pounds. Not bad, as I had only been in the place for about ten or fifteen minutes. I tucked the money into the front pocket of my jeans and then went to find Shane. I decided not to tell him about the money. There might be a code among thieves, but I wasn't going to keep it, not tonight anyway! I told Shane that I hadn't found anything and that as the place was giving him the creeps we would leave. Shane readily agreed, as he had no stomach for the break-in anyhow.

That night was another milestone in my callous criminal career. Although I hadn't actually robbed the dead, I had been prepared to do so, and probably would have done if I hadn't struck it rich in the office drawer.

The next day, I was amused to watch the television news, which had reported the burglary in depth, explaining that thieves had received a shock when they broke into the funeral home the night before. They knew this because they had left the fridge door wide open!

House Burglary

Breaking into shops, offices and clubs was one thing, but as my crime spree with Shane escalated, we fixed our sights on people's homes. Shane continued to borrow the Triumph Dolomite from his homosexual friend. I never asked him whether their friendship had become physical, and to be honest I didn't care. As long as we could use the guy's car, it didn't matter. The car was handy, as we found we could go out to more remote homes and, once we established that they were empty, we could strike.

Going through people's drawers and personal effects didn't bother me at all. I had started all those years before at Mr and Mrs Smith's, and progressed from there. Normally we would stick together in one room, searching quickly with our eyes and gloved hands for anything that we might be able to sell or use ourselves. In the week before my last and final arrest, we broke into a few houses every night. I remember in one isolated country house finding a shotgun in the hallway. We sat down in the owner's lounge and enjoyed their Southern Comfort, swigging it straight from the bottle. It was then that I thought of my next plan. We would steal the shotgun and saw off the barrel, and then we could start robbing post offices in the rural areas of Dorset and Hampshire.

The plan was just coming together when we heard the sound of tyres on gravel and saw the headlights of a car through the thin curtains. Like startled rabbits, we dived for the back door, which we had already opened from the inside, and then we were gone, hidden by the darkness of the night. Once we had scrambled into the car, which was parked up the lane, I realised that I had left the gun behind. It was too late, and now it was time to head back to Liz's. That was close, but I'd had many close encounters in my sordid life of deceit and crime, and my escape was not down to luck, but experience, or so I fooled myself.

Undeterred by the night before, Shane and I headed again for the forest area. This time, foolishly, we had drunk a quantity of Scotch and were pretty intoxicated. Thankfully, the roads were empty as we closed in on our next target.

This was a house that Shane had broken into sometime before and had been caught! Shane, however, was convinced that there was much jewellery to be had, as the occupier was a rich, single old woman. Standing in the garden, I began to feel nervous. This was not like me, but I sensed that something was wrong. Shane came around the side of the building. He said that he thought the house was empty and that we had better strike now before anyone turned up. With a gloved fist I smashed through a hall window and was in the house within seconds, although a little wobbly because of the drink I had consumed. Shane was hot on my tail when it all turned horribly wrong.

> *With a gloved fist I smashed through a hall window and was in the house within seconds, although a little wobbly because of the drink I had consumed. Shane was hot on my tail when it all turned horribly wrong*

The door of the lounge opened, and an old lady appeared and began to order us out of her home. I told her not to worry as we were going. She then said she felt ill and we, thinking she might collapse, decided she should lie down and so we helped her to her bedroom. Once we had made her comfortable we knew we had blown it – a house with somebody in! That was never our plan and now we had to escape quickly. Running down the stairs, we ran for the front door and were gone in a flash. The lady, a brave soul, called for help, and so the police were alerted. This was serious, as now the burglary was aggravated by the fact that somebody was at home and had challenged us.

You Can Run But You Can't Hide

It was just a question of time before the police caught up with Shane. The lady had recognised him from a court appearance some time ago. They had picked him up early in the morning and were interviewing him as I was eating my breakfast. It didn't take Sherlock Holmes to work out that serial burglars were operating in that area – and we were in the frame. They also knew, through the woman's testimony, that there were two men involved. Now they were going to work on Shane to find out who the other man was. Although the lady was not hurt in any way and although I had helped her to her room when she felt ill, which was a ploy on her part that worked, it still left the fact that a serious crime had been committed. Given the fact that a string of houses had suffered the same fate, the police threatened Shane with a long custodial sentence. On the other hand, if he co-operated with their inquiries, they would take all that into consideration at his court appearance. It worked, and Shane sang like a little nightingale, giving the police all the information needed to arrest me and give me a tough interrogation. In fact, he basically suggested that I had forced him into the dirty deed, which was rich considering he planned the hit and actually drove me there, as I couldn't even drive!

I went to work as usual that morning. As a butcher, at a small shop by Poole Quay, I was working on a piece of beef with a boning knife in my hand, when the door opened and in walked two men wearing suits. They asked me if I was Richard Pidgley, and when I replied that I was, they asked me to put my knife down. I did so and they arrested me, reciting the statutory caution. Within moments, two more CID officers came running into the shop from the back entrance. I was handcuffed and bundled into an unmarked police car and driven directly to Poole police station. I was taken to the charging room, frisked thoroughly and made to sign for all my personal effects.

Some CID officers, who had travelled from Ringwood to interview Shane, now wanted to see me, so I was marched into an interview room. The process had begun, and although I had talked and walked from the police before, this time I knew it wasn't going to happen. They knew too many details, and even though I didn't want to think it, I had to accept that Shane had probably grassed me up. After hours of talking, the Forest CID signed for me and under the cover of night drove me to Ringwood police station, where it all started again. I remember looking at the clock on the wall, it was now the early hours and I hadn't admitted anything, but the pressure was beginning to take its toll, as I could hardly keep my eyes open. Finally, I was taken to the cells, which were very old-fashioned and sparse. A thin blanket was all I had to keep me warm through the night.

The next morning as I woke up, my body was craving for a cigarette, but there was no chance of that luxury, not as long as I refused to co-operate with the police. I had a full bladder and needed the toilet. So, feeling miserable, I began to boot the door with my bare feet, as my shoes had been removed. Just when I thought I was going to have to use the cell wall as a urinal, a big uniformed officer entered the small cellblock and began to swear at me for making such a racket so early in the morning. The door opened and he pointed to a dank toilet at the end of the corridor. The officer stood watching me as I used the toilet. I hated that indignity, but I knew I would have to get used to it, because in captivity there is no privacy.

After I had been served breakfast, brought into the station from the bed and breakfast across the road, I was taken into the interview room. The day started with intensive interrogations, and although I kept up my defence, I now realised I was in big trouble and nothing I could do would avert the inevitable.

Shane had told the police just about everything there was to know. By their questioning I knew there was little point in holding out, but I was aware that it was better to be remanded in custody as an unconvicted prisoner, than a convicted one, so I kept quiet and frustrated the police as much as I could.

In the interview room I sat behind a desk, with three officers in the room with me. Once the interview was terminated they went to take me back to my cell. Being rebellious, I defied them, refusing to go. At that they came for me. I had nothing to lose by now, so I kicked over the big wooden table between us and backed into the corner of the room where the breathalysing equipment was stored. I didn't stand a chance against three large Hampshire policemen, but it was worth a go and brought a bit of relief to the boredom of the interview. I punched and kicked, and they gave as good back. Eventually, more policemen bundled into the room, and they carried me back to the cell block, throwing me into my cell with a torrent of verbal abuse.

That night, Shane was brought to the same police station and we talked through the flaps in the cell doors. Although Shane denied grassing me up, I knew it was him. For now it would have to wait, but I determined that vengeance would be mine someday.

That same night, I was marched back into the Ringwood interview room and formally charged with a string of burglaries. Going back to my cell, I thought about all I had done and, with a sigh, I accepted the fact that, 'if you do the crime, you do the time'. Shivering in the cold dark cell, as I drifted into sleep, I welcomed myself to the new world I would be living in for quite some time. A world of locks and keys; a world of absolute captivity; a place where I ceased being a human being with a name but became a prisoner with a number, languishing behind those cold bars, serving out my sentence until every day was paid in full.

If you do the crime, you do the time

Goodbye Liberty – Hello Captivity!

The next day was Saturday, and with much security Shane and I were handcuffed to two large policemen and driven to Ringwood Magistrates' Court. The room was large and bare, nothing like the grand courtrooms belonging to the Crown at Poole or Bournemouth. The court had about fifteen people inside when we arrived, with three of those sitting behind a table at the front of the room. We sat between the two policemen in front of the magistrates. The clerk read the charges out and we were asked how we pleaded. Both of us pleaded 'Not guilty', which was a joke for Shane as he had confessed everything already to the police at his arrest. The chairman of the magistrates talked quietly to his two colleagues and then told the court that the two prisoners would be remanded in custody at Dorchester prison for a fortnight while reports were being compiled.

As we were led into the foyer of the courthouse, the policemen we were handcuffed to removed the cuffs and then handcuffed Shane and I together. While this was happening, a police transit van or 'meat wagon' as the cons used to call them, was driven onto the forecourt of the court building. This was our chance of escape. I whispered to Shane that we ought to make a run for it and so, as we were led outside into the sunshine, we broke away from the grip of the policemen. Then, all hell broke loose, as the police panicked, fearful of losing two prisoners. The plan was doomed from the beginning, but it was worth having a go. Officers tackled us to the ground and in the struggle I received a bloody nose and scratched face. The doors of the police van were flung open and we were literally thrown head first into the back of the van. One of the officers who climbed in with us tightened the handcuffs to the extent that the blood supply almost stopped flowing into our hands. As the cuffs dug deep into our wrists we were told to 'behave or else'. When we agreed to sit properly and not try any more tricks, the handcuffs were finally loosened.

Then, all hell broke loose, as the police panicked

Looking out of the window, I gazed at the beautiful Dorset countryside on my way to Dorchester prison. Up until now I had never appreciated it, because my seedy world of sin and crime had blinded me to the beauty staring at me in the face all the time. Stripped of everything, including my very liberty, I began to long for the freedom of just walking down a country lane and listening to the birds singing: a pleasure that costs nothing but would now elude me for literally years.

As we rolled up to the great gates of Dorchester prison, situated in Barrack square, just a stone's throw from the centre of Dorchester itself, I felt a sense of despair flood my thoughts. I was entering another world. People walking about in the street outside would forget me. Who cares about prisoners? I could die in there and it wouldn't matter to anybody at all.

By now I was like an 'old lag' at the age of 17. I hated induction, but knew the ropes all too well: standing naked in front of the screws and the indignity of the officers checking every part of your anatomy for concealed drugs; the paperwork that took forever; the bath; the rough towels; the prison uniform that was always too large and shoes that never fitted properly; waiting in a holding cell with nothing to do until a prison officer took you into the main prison block. Yes, I hated induction, but I would have to accept whatever came to me in this world of locks and bars.

After being processed through induction I was taken to a cell with Shane. This time, because of space problems in the Youth Wing, we were placed on the ground floor by the main food-serving area. This turned out to be a good location, as we got our meals first, and as the older convicts serving up the prison food called us 'Baby Burglars', we normally got a good portion of piping hot food.

The next morning, after breakfast, I was escorted to the Principal Officer's office. Once inside and the door shut, the officer went through all the details of my case and then told me my prison number, J52327. From then on, I was a number and no longer a person. The luxury of a first name is unheard of in prison; every time I had to report to a prison officer I had to say, 'J52327 Pidgley, Sir.'

My name was all I had left. Everything else had been taken from me, and so the final act of dehumanising me had taken place. I would no longer be called Richard until months later, when I began to have a regular prison visitor come to see me at Aylesbury.

After that first fortnight at Dorchester, we were driven back to Ringwood Magistrates' Court for another hearing. This was a waste of time for us, because we had to go through the procedure

> *The officer went through all the details of my case and then told me my prison number, J52327. From then on, I was a number and no longer a person*

of paperwork and being processed for the court appearance. It was a waste of time, because the court promptly sent us back to prison on remand for yet another fortnight, while reports were still being compiled. At least we got out of our cell and had a day's ride through the New Forest! No wonder the taxpayer gets so irate at the wastage of the nation's financial resources when it's funding prisoners' day trips.

I'd had the inner strength to get through my time in prison before, but this time things all got too much for me. For a start, I had no idea how long I would have to wait until my court appearance which, because of my previous criminal record, was now certainly going to be at Bournemouth Crown Court. And secondly, I was angry with Shane for grassing me up to the police. He was still denying it, but I knew he had done it, and the smouldering fire of revenge in my heart was being fanned by the wind of anger, day by day. In the end I got to the stage where I felt I could not eat, such was the anger inside me towards Shane. For a fortnight, I collected my food and then threw it out of the window for the birds, because my appetite was gone. It was replaced by awful visions of violent vengeance on Shane.

I had this daily waking dream of following Shane into a room, away from other people, and then plunging a butcher's boning knife into his abdomen, slicing through his liver and kidneys. I could feel his hot blood on my hands as it spurted and pumped out all over my clothes. The daily vision of murdering Shane gave me hope; hope that I would one day be released to exact such a terrible revenge upon the man I had once considered a friend. I made my secret plans to get Shane, and meditated upon them daily, considering where and when I would strike and then how I would fix an alibi and use a fire to burn all my bloodstained clothes.

> *Plunging a butcher's boning knife into his abdomen, slicing through his liver and kidneys. I could feel his hot blood on my hands as it spurted and pumped out all over my clothes*

Day by day the vision became clearer, and nearly became a reality as, one day, after dinner, Shane and I fell out and I exploded angrily and violently.

Shane had said something and that had set me off. Within a split second I had leapt from my bunk to his in our small cell and was grappling with him. My hands now around his throat, I began to squeeze the very life breath out of him. As he frantically fought for air, he got lucky as his right hand smashed into the emergency bell on the cell wall by the door. I continued to fight with

Shane as we crashed to the floor, still with my hands fixed firmly around his throat. It was a small miracle for me that the door opened, and prison officers rushed in, dragging me off Shane. If they had not intervened, I could well have been in prison to this very day serving a life sentence for murder!

It was obvious that I was the one who had started the fight, and so I was roughly marched to a dungeon cell in the prison. The punishment block, or dungeon as we called it, was built at a lower level than the other ground-floor cells. In fact, the window was very high up in the cell wall, with bars that were almost on the outside ground level. This made the room very dark and oppressive, and led to despair in any captive inside. I was flung in with a torrent of threats from the screws as they slammed the door shut on me.

As I sank to the floor, I felt absolutely alone and totally isolated, knowing that I could be in there for days, languishing in those dark, dank and depressive surrounds. Up to this point, I had been the big mouth, the rebel, but now I felt rotten and so empty inside. My life flashed before my eyes: everything came back to me in my mind like a slide show, and I felt that my whole life was a waste of space. I was empty, I was ruined, and I had nothing in the world. Talk about poor: I didn't even have a name, just a prison number. I didn't know how long I was going to be in the dungeon, and I honestly felt that I could no longer cope with life. Nobody loved me or cared about me, and as far as the screws were concerned I was worthless scum.

Such darkness flooded my soul then, that suicide seemed the only way out. There was a real presence of evil and darkness in that cell; an evil that seemed to put me under a spell. The devil had no more use for me now, so his last action would be to destroy me. Enough was enough. A sickening sense of lostness and failure flooded my already dark, cold and empty heart. In a moment I had lost the will to live. As I reflected on seventeen years, I realised that I was a waster, a nobody going nowhere, and I wanted out.

As if in a trance I ripped the sheet off the bed. I rolled the sheet up into a makeshift rope, tying one end in a slip-knot and then binding the other end to the bars in the small window high up on the cell wall. I stood on the radiator pipe with the rope around my neck and I tottered forward into a certain and most painful death of suffocation. And then it happened! I can't fully explain it, but it seemed as if a strong, powerful and yet invisible hand pushed me back against the cell wall. The hand, if it was a hand, then lifted the rope from my neck and let me slide gently to the floor.

> *I stood on the radiator pipe with the rope around my neck and I tottered forward*

I don't know how much later it was, but finally the door opened and prison officers rushed in. On seeing the rope still attached to the prison bars, they stripped me naked and forced some medicine down my throat. Then they put me into a padded cell, still naked, with a sort of quilted blanket as my only source of covering and warmth. Later, I realised that God had saved me from suicide and a certain hell.

The Power of Prayer

Much later, I was amazed to hear that my strange experience in the Dorchester dungeon was an extraordinary answer to prayer. Somebody at a large Baptist church in

Bournemouth had read about my case in the local paper. Reading the details of my disturbing case history, they realised my life was broken and empty. Then, with a real concern for me, because I was in so much trouble, they told the other members of the church about my situation and they all started praying for me.

God heard the faithful prayers of those people who cared about me, even though they didn't know me. They had actually been praying for me at the time I was in the dungeon cell! Little did they know that God would not only save me from suicide, but also save me from my sins and call me to the ministry. That's why the Bible also encourages us to pray by saying, '*Now glory be to God! By his mighty power at work within us, he is able to accomplish infinitely more than we would ever dare to ask or hope.*'[6]

After the suicide attempt, I was escorted to Winchester prison. The prison was known for its very large hospital wing, which caged some strange prisoners indeed, including me!

Once I was processed at Winchester, I was taken to my cell, which was actually quite pleasant. Well, pleasant after the dungeon and padded cell I had found myself in just days before. An officer and two inmates brought meals to my cell. Talk about room service! Yet all was not good, as that place was full of darkness and depression. As I got to slop out my chamber pot that night just before lights out, I saw, briefly, a young man in the cell adjoining mine. Early the next morning there was a lot of confusion outside my neighbouring cell. The young man who I had seen hours before was being cut down and his

> *The young man who I had seen hours before was being cut down and his corpse removed from the cell*

corpse removed from the cell. That hospital wing was reserved for the crazy and suicidal and I was in the midst of it all. Although the cell was nice, light and warm, the atmosphere was awful, with a depressive heaviness that seemed to soak into everything.

After a week, one morning I was told that I was going to the 'Doll's House', which was the nickname for the Youth Wing of Winchester prison. Settling into my new cell, I soon made friends with the other young man who would be sharing the same air and space for the foreseeable future. The days went quickly in the Doll's House. I was given the job of cleaning the 'M1', which was the main corridor that ran along the whole length of the Youth Wing block. The job got me out of my cell for most of the morning, which was a welcome break from the confines of a small two-man cell. The floor had to be swept, mopped and then polished to a sparkling shine so that you could almost see your face in it.

My barrister came to see me at Winchester. He told me very plainly that I didn't stand a chance pleading 'Not guilty'. It would be better for me if I took it like a man and owned up to what he knew I had done. I realised that he was right and so agreed to his counsel. He warned me that I would probably get a long sentence because of the way I had openly broken the community service imposed upon me at my last appearance at Bournemouth Crown Court. I knew that I was in for the high jump this time, and so mentally prepared myself for the worst, which could be years inside prison.

The Sentence

By now, Shane had also been brought to the Doll's House, and the day of our court appearance came. We were handcuffed together and escorted under guard from Winchester prison to Bournemouth Crown Court in a transit van. The van went straight to the prisoners' entrance, which was below ground level. In the underground cells, we waited for our case to be called. By now I was feeling nervous, and a cold sweat broke out all over my body. Shivering in my cell I finally heard footsteps coming towards me. Both Shane and I were warned about attempting to escape and how futile it would be. Then we climbed two flights of narrow stairs onto a landing. There was a small flight of steps still to climb, which led directly into the dock. We were like actors in the wings of a theatre waiting for our cue. The signal was given and we climbed the last steps into the dock and surveyed the half-full courtroom.

The clerk said, 'Court rise,' and we all stood as three robed and wigged men walked from a side door into the courtroom and took their place at the bench. Our names were read out, and we had to answer to them. Then, all the charges were read out. They seemed to go on and on, and the newspaper reporter probably had a job to scribble it all down. Once the charges were read out, we then had to let it be known to the court how we were going to plead, 'Guilty' or 'Not guilty'. As I stood before the judges, I was horrified to see that the one sitting to the right was the same judge who had sentenced me to community service only months earlier. He had warned me that if I ever came into his court again he would give me the maximum sentence. I knew that it was hopeless to try to talk my way out of the situation and impossible to escape, as there were two prison officers in the dock and policemen at the court door. Resigning myself to whatever would happen next, I pleaded 'Guilty'. I sat down, and the next few hours all seemed to be a blur.

Finally, after much reviewing of all I had done, I was asked if I had anything to say. I rose to my feet and began to apologise for everything I had done; saying sorry to all the people I had committed crimes against. The judges then retired to consider the sentencing, and I was taken back down to my cell in the basement of the building.

I was no longer feeling afraid at this point. After all, there was absolutely nothing I could do to alter things, and the clock could never be turned back. So I waited in my cell. One of the screws – a friendly one – came along and joked that I only had to worry if the judge came back in with a black cap on! He gave me a cigarette, and as I smoked it, suddenly we were called back up to the court. The clerk said his customary 'Court rise' and we all stood to our feet again. When the judges had taken their place at the bench everyone was asked to sit.

Then the judge seated in the middle asked me to stand and he proceeded to formally sentence me. I can't remember all he said, but the words 'four years' kept ringing in my head. Four years, can you imagine being sentenced to four years in prison? Whether you deserve it or not, four years is still a long stretch for a young person to come to terms with. The only thing that softened that mighty blow was that when Shane was asked to stand, he, too, was sentenced to four years' imprisonment.

I finally felt that justice, in a strange sort of way, had been done. The man who had grassed me up to the police, thinking he would get off with a lighter sentence, was given the same as me! The joy of knowing that he, too, would have to do his 'bird' (prison slang for time in jail), brought immense comfort to me as I skipped down the steps, returning to my basement cell. That night, after tea in the prison cells at Bournemouth Crown Court, we were escorted under guard once again to Dorchester prison. The induction process over, we were taken to the same cell that we had been in weeks before. So much had happened that day that I really didn't have the energy to worry about the implications of such a long sentence. I put my head upon my pillow and fell asleep.

The next day I was marched into the Principal Officer's office, and he went through the details of my sentencing, explaining that if I behaved myself in prison I could be out after maybe two and a half years. I was also told that because I was now doing a long prison stretch, Dorchester prison could no longer house me, and so I was being transferred the next day to Aylesbury Youth Custody Centre, where I would serve the rest of my sentence.

8

THE GREATEST DISCOVERY

The long drive from Dorchester prison to Aylesbury Youth Custody Centre was a joy. Beautiful fields and trees flanked the roadsides and, as the prison van sped on its way, cutting through the countryside, I drank in all I could see, marvelling at the vast open spaces after the confines of Dorchester's exercise yard.

I had never been into the county of Buckinghamshire before, and now here I was being driven under escort, all courtesy of Her Majesty the Queen! The four screws were in a good mood: the escort duty broke up the daily monotony of herding prisoners in and out of different cellblocks. They actually gave us a few cigarettes to smoke on the journey, which was normally unheard of in the prison.

I had a feeling that all was going to be well at Aylesbury Youth Custody Centre, unlike the despairing feeling of Dorchester prison. I didn't know it then, but I was about to make the greatest discovery of my lifetime – a discovery so great that it would change my life forever!

As the prison van drove into Aylesbury, approaching the prison gates along the main road, I tried to retain a mental picture of the outside of the prison. I looked long and hard at those impregnable walls topped with razor wire, and those great wooden and iron gates, making the place a fortress to the outside world and keeping me inside as a prisoner for what might well be a period of three years. The driver sounded the horn and a small door opened in the left-hand door of the great gates. A prison officer emerged and took the details from our driver. Moments later, the gates opened and in we drove. That was the last time I would see the real world for years.

> *I looked long and hard at those impregnable walls topped with razor wire*

The gatehouse consisted of two great gates, with enough space in between for a minibus to park. They were never opened at the same time in case some prisoner felt the temptation to break the 100 metres sprint record! However, a year on from that day I did get to see both gates opened at once.

It happened one day while I was cleaning the chief officers' corridor as a trusted prisoner. The fire alarm had gone off and two fire engines came, as was procedure, alerted by the sirens. I gazed through the open door of the main office block and, for a moment, saw the outside world, as the engines screamed through the gatehouse.

Induction

Induction at Aylesbury was no different to that at any other prison in which I had been. Standing in front of the induction officers, I had to strip off all my clothes and go through the same humiliation as before. The bathhouse was pleasant though. It was through a door into a different room, and because there were only Shane and me to be 'processed', there was no rush to be 'sheep-dipped'. I sank into the warm water of the bath and enjoyed those moments immensely, away from the ever-watchful eyes of prison officers. You get only one bath when you go to prison, and that's when you get processed in the induction wing. After that, it's a shower once a week for a maximum of five minutes, if you're lucky.

I could have soaked for hours, but it wasn't to be, as the induction officer told us to hurry up. Once dried off – and this time with the modesty of a towel wrapped around my middle – I was led to a third room filled with shelves of prison clothing. I was asked my size, and amazingly, they actually found clothes that fitted me. Second-hand, of course, but at least they fitted! White underpants, woollen socks, a faded blue tee shirt, blue denim jeans with a matching denim jacket and a pair of black shoes. I was also kitted out with a plastic knife, fork and spoon set, a plastic mug, a towel, a comb and a pair of pyjamas. Armed with all my new things, I was ordered to follow the officer onto the upstairs landing of the induction wing.

There were ten cells along that landing, each designed to house one prisoner while they served their two weeks of induction training at Aylesbury prison. My cell was spartan, with one bed, a small cupboard unit with a drawer, cupboard and towel rail, a plastic jug, washbowl and toilet pot – thankfully fitted with a lid. I was told to make myself at home, for presently someone would be along to see me. In fact, over the next few days, I saw quite a few different people associated with the prison. The assistant governor came along, one of the principal officers, a psychoanalyst (probably to confirm I was crazy!), the chaplain, the doctor and the wing officer. The wing officer was quite strict, and as he went through all the rules for me, he told me that nobody had escaped from the prison, and if he caught me trying to, he would personally break my arms and legs! After our 'friendly' chat, I decided there and then I wouldn't ever try to escape.

Induction is hated by most of the cons (prisoners) because it means you are locked up for long periods of time with nothing to relieve the boredom. In fact, you only get to leave your cell for the three daily meal times. Even then you only have to go down a flight of stairs into the main prison area and collect your food from a serving bay. Once you had eaten your food it was back to your cell again for more 'bang up', as we called it. If the weather was good, we were able to go into the bottom exercise yard for a walk, but that was only for half an hour. Because of bad weather, we were only able to go out there about three times in the fortnight I was held on the induction wing. Induction was also hated because you were deprived of the right to work, so you couldn't earn any money, and without money you are helpless if you want to buy cigarettes, which is what almost every con craves.

The prison authority didn't want a riot on their hands though, so they graciously gave every prisoner on induction about £1.03 per week. With that, you had just enough money to buy half an ounce of Old Holborn rolling tobacco, a packet of Rizlas (cigarette papers) and a box of safety matches. In the interest of security the Swan Vesta type were banned, due to their explosive nature. The problem was that you had to roll the cigarettes very thin to make the 'burn' (prison slang for tobacco) last you the whole week – which took great discipline. Also, the matches always ran out. To overcome that problem every con learns the art of match-splitting. Taking a razor, you carefully splice the match into two and then, for the experienced lag – as I had become – you do it a second time. A box of 40 matches now becomes a box of 160. Sometimes the head of the match would fall off the splinter to which it was attached, and that would make things very tricky. You can't stick it back on, not in prison anyway. It happened to me on many occasions, often when it was late at night and it was the only match I had left. Now that's a disaster!

Craving for nicotine and having a broken match means one thing – satisfaction only comes through pain. With a sweaty fingertip pressed into the broken incendiary of the match head and the cigarette in your mouth, you use your finger as the match. You have a split second to ignite the cigarette and draw on the smoke as the match literally lights up on the end of your finger, burning the flesh in sharp pain. Such was my deep dependence on nicotine, I would often resort to such emergency tactics to have a smoke. Often, through prison days when I had run out of 'burn', I would walk along the corridors with my eyes to the ground like an eagle. If I saw the butt end of a stamped out cigarette, I would swoop down to pick it up, grovelling and humiliating myself as I would later smoke the butt end to feed my powerful habit.

Thinking back, I remembered saying that I could quit smoking at any time. Yet, at that time I was reduced to such levels of depravity to satisfy the hunger and need for nicotine. Young people are seduced by the cool and sexy look of blue smoke exhaled by the smoker, unaware of the vice-like grip it places upon its unsuspecting victim. Yes, induction was a killer, but if you could mentally endure its painful boredom you stood a chance of doing your bird.

After all the interviews had taken place, I resigned myself to the incredible boredom that was now to come. Sitting on my bunk, I looked around my new cell. There were a few items that had already caught my eye: the cupboard in which to put my towel and spare underwear, a plastic water jug and mug, a washbowl and a toilet pot – nothing else. No cigarettes, no magazines, in fact, nothing at all. Then I spotted a red book that was lying on the floor by the cupboard. I wasn't in the mood for reading, but anything was better than the desperate craving for nicotine, or going insane with boredom. I looked at the book, and to my disgust saw that it was a Gideon

I looked at the book, and to my disgust saw that it was a Gideon Bible!

Bible! Without thinking, I stretched from my bunk and took the Bible from the floor.

Something strange happened as I picked up the Gideon Bible: I actually had this inexplicable desire to read it. This was alien to me, as I had never desired to read the Bible before. I had stolen a Bible once, from Operation Mobilisation's boat *Logos* as she was berthed at Poole Quay, when I was at the children's home, but when I couldn't sell it to anyone I simply heaved it into a skip by the side of the road.

I began to read the Bible, starting in one of the Gospels purely by chance and not by choice, as this was where the Bible had opened when I picked it up. I read about the man called Jesus Christ, who was doing amazing things. He actually healed people: the blind received their sight and the lame leapt for joy as Jesus' power made them well. Amazing as it seemed, I read about Jesus doing the impossible like raising the dead. In fact, those Bible pages were full of and focused on all the incredible miracles that Jesus performed. Best of all, Jesus was seen to be making time for people who were considered outcasts by everyone else. Could I be reading right?

I didn't need to be a theologian to understand that God wasn't happy with my behaviour. In fact, God's son, Jesus Christ, went to great lengths to teach righteous living and was quick to condemn sin! As my eyes soaked up those golden words, I grasped this wonderful truth: God loved me and he wanted me to give up my wretched, poor lifestyle so that I could receive his forgiveness. This was amazing! The words that I read and re-read burned in my heart: in fact, I couldn't put the Bible down. I'd had powerful experiences of the dark occult world. I knew the intoxicating power of liquor and the rush and euphoria that drugs had brought into my life, but this Bible was something else! I had never touched anything like this before: the Bible seemed to be a living book and I was compelled to keep reading page after page after page.

Revelation

As I read the Bible, the verses came alive to me. One such verse that deeply touched my heart was from the Gospel of John, when Jesus spoke about the love of God to a religious man hungry for spiritual truth. *'For God so loved the world that he gave his only Son, so that everyone who believes in him will not perish but have eternal life.'*[7]

Revelation dawned upon the darkness of my soul. Yes, God loved me! I couldn't get that amazing fact out of my mind. Yes, God Almighty, the Creator of Heaven and Earth, actually loved a lowlife such as me!

I later understood the wonderful words of the hymn writer, C. H. Gabriel, who wrote

I stand amazed in the presence of Jesus the Nazarene,
And wonder how he could love me, a sinner, condemned, unclean.
Oh how marvellous! Oh how wonderful! And my song shall
    ever be;
Oh how marvellous! Oh how wonderful! Is my Saviour's love
    for me!

As I read about the earthly ministry of Jesus Christ among ordinary people I was amazed. Now, however, the Gospel account began to rise to a dramatic climax as Jesus was arrested, tried and cruelly crucified on a wooden cross. At his arrest Jesus said that he could have called on thousands of angels to rescue him, but he didn't. Jesus knew only too well that his death on the cross was all part of God's plan to bring man back to himself from the dark paths of sin. The Bible explained that Jesus' death on the cross was all about God loving me, and proving that love, by taking the punishment I rightly deserved for all the wrong I had ever done.

The cross of Jesus Christ made a deep impact on my life. Love, so I am told, can be measured by what someone is prepared to give, or give up, for another person. The television commercial cashes in on this with the now famous advert for the Nestlé chocolate company's product 'Rolos': with the two little sweethearts and the final catch phrase, 'Do you love anyone enough to give them your last Rolo?' Well God did love us, enough to give us his only son to die in our place. This was love not merely in words, which we all know can

The cross of Jesus Christ made a deep impact on my life

mean very little, but a powerful demonstration of God's love that would change the history of the world.

Years later, a preacher illustrated this wonderful truth by telling a story about a bridge-keeper in Germany who had the responsibility of operating a large rail swing-bridge over a river. The keeper, on being alerted of a train approaching, would use great gear wheels kept in a pit to move the massive bridge into the right position spanning the river, thus allowing a train to pass over the water safely. The keeper would salute the passing train with all its city passengers on their way home from work and they would wave back to him.

One day during the school holidays, his son, a young boy, went to watch his dad at work. Being alerted to a train speeding towards the bridge, the dad went, as usual, to operate the machinery that moved the bridge into position. Almost immediately, he heard a pitiful scream as he pulled a gear lever. It had come from the pit containing the massive gear wheels. Running to the pit, he looked down and to his sickening horror saw his young son helplessly entangled in the mechanism.

The keeper knew that it would take many men, and probably hours, to free the trapped boy and there was no time. Unless he moved the bridge, the train would go crashing into the river, causing great loss of life; if he did move the bridge it would kill his son. The agonising decision was made instantly. With a pain that threatened to rip out his own heart, the bridge-keeper moved the bridge and crushed the life out of his beloved small son. With seconds to spare, the bridge was positioned as the train came rumbling down the track. The whistle blew, the engine driver and fireman waved and the people waved as usual to the keeper. They couldn't see the hot tears streaming down his face soaking his beard. 'Don't they know about my son?' thought the keeper as the train sped away to its destination.

There came a day in heaven when God, the divine 'bridge-keeper', seeing the 'train' full of fallen mankind fast approaching the 'river of judgement and death', leapt into action and allowed his son to die sacrificially in our place. We should have paid for our own sins by dying the death God's holiness and righteousness requires. Yet God paid for us all.

The Bible records God's unchanging character as love. The Apostle John wrote to the first Christians telling them 'God is love'. Jesus, himself, as he approached Jerusalem, the city of his execution, knowing the full horror of what awaited him at the cross, said to his disciples, *'Greater love hath no man than this, that a man lay down his life for his friends.'* [8]

I didn't have to be a Bible college student to understand that God not only deeply loved me, but also wanted me to turn from my sinful lifestyle in sincere repentance. God wanted me to enjoy a whole new life through his son, Jesus Christ, who was the only way to eternal life. As the days went by, I kept reading the Bible. Things that used to intimidate me, such as my cramped cell with its oppressive bars, and the prison officers, no longer bothered me at all, as I was now totally absorbed by the Gideon Bible I had found in my cell.

Induction passed quickly and before I knew it I was transferred to the second landing of A wing known as A2. As I bundled my things together and followed the senior officer into the main prison block, the Gideon Bible came with me. I had found true treasure in the Bible, and I wasn't going to let go of it at any cost.

Salvation Immense and Free

One night, 19th December 1984, as I was reading the Bible before the lights went out, the words from the Apostle John's first letter hit me straight between the eyes:

> *This is the message he has given us to announce to you: God is light and there is no darkness in him at all. So we are lying if we say we have fellowship with God but go on living in spiritual darkness. We are not living in the truth. But if we are living in the light of God's presence, just as Christ is, then we have fellowship with each other, and the blood of Jesus, his Son, cleanses us from every sin. If we say we have no sin, we are only fooling ourselves and refusing to accept the truth. But if we confess our sins to him, he is faithful and just to forgive us and to cleanse us from every wrong.*[9]

That was it, I knew I had to get right with God and ask Christ into my heart to be my Saviour. Up until that point, nobody had ever preached to me, nor had anyone ever counselled me, but the Word of God, which is living and active, worked deep down in my life. Each word was like a beam of light bringing life and light into the darkness of my sinful being. Behind the high walls of this prison in Aylesbury, I had encountered the Living God in my small prison cell through his eternal Word, the Bible. That night I got on my knees, on the cold hard floor and began to cry out to God. I didn't really know how to pray, but then as one modern Bible translation puts it, '*And when you come before God, don't turn that*

> *That was it, I knew I had to get right with God and ask Christ into my heart to be my Saviour*

into a theatrical production either. All these people making a regular show out of their prayers, hoping for stardom! Do you think God sits in a box seat? Here's what you should do: find a quiet, secluded place so you won't be tempted to role-play before God. Just be there as simply and honestly as you can manage. The focus will shift from you to God, and you will begin to sense his grace.'[10]

That's how everyone should pray – being totally honest with the God who created you, focusing on his love for you and his willingness to listen to all those who call on his name in sincerity, believing he will hear and answer prayer. And so I, for the first time ever in my life cried out to God. I held nothing back as I confessed all my filthy, rotten sins that had separated me from God; sins that had robbed me of life for more than eighteen years.

My sins had caused much suffering to the one who was perfect and absolutely holy. There is no love like the love of God, and I knew that the emptiness and pain of all my years was now over. For at the cross of Jesus Christ there was hope. Tears began to flow down my cheeks as I realised what a mess my life was in before God's holy and awesome presence. Yes, the tears flowed freely as I grasped the reality of Jesus' awful pain and death upon the cross, which was endured for sinners such as me to buy my freedom from emptiness and death.

Salvation is not something we achieve, but rather something we receive

The truth is, salvation is not something we achieve, but rather something we receive. So at the foot of the cross, looking by faith to Jesus Christ, I received the forgiveness of God and a whole new life. God heard my cry of repentance and faith, as he promises to hear any who call to him.

Those were precious moments indeed for me in my prison cell, for as I basked in the light of God's grace and mercy, angel choirs sang the praises of a saving God in heaven. It was then, at that moment, Jesus Christ, the Son of God did two wonderful things for me.

Firstly, he wrote my name in his 'Book of Life'.[11] My name had been recorded at New Scotland Yard, along with my fingerprints, and probably still is, as a felon. However, in heaven there is a book, the greatest book in the universe, called 'The Book of Life', and my name was recorded in that book the instant I repented and believed in Jesus Christ as my Saviour. If you are ever granted the privilege of turning the pages of that celestial book, turn to 19th December 1984. Cast your eye down the page and you will see my name, 'Richard Pidgley', and by the side of it written the wonderful word that summed up my experience, 'Forgiven'.

Secondly, not only did the Son of God write my name in his 'Book of Life', but he also came into my heart. For too long, God was at a distance, but now he was with me and in me. Jesus said, *'Look! Here I stand at the door and knock. If you hear me calling and open the door, I will come in, and we will share a meal as friends.'*[12]

The world-famous painter, Holman Hunt, captured that scripture with his great renowned painting, 'The Light of the World' where Jesus is portrayed standing outside an old, weed overgrown door, holding a lamp in his hand. There is no handle on the outside, signifying that if Christ is to gain entry, it can only be initiated by us opening the door from the inside. Although God is sovereign and all-powerful and he can do anything he wants, he created us with free will so that we can make up our own minds about him. God doesn't force himself upon people but he knocks on the door of every heart: sometimes through the Bible, other times through preaching in churches, or a radio or television programme. Some people hear God knocking when friends testify about God's grace and their Saviour Jesus Christ.

For years I failed to hear the knocking of a persistent Saviour, but now, I am sure glad that the day came when I heard him loud and clear and threw open the door of my heart allowing him free access to all that I am.

Instantly, I knew that I was saved! This was not mere emotion, although I was very emotional and tearful, but rather a faith focused on the work Jesus Christ accomplished by dying on the cross for my sins and rising from the dead on the third day for my justification.

People aren't saved through emotions, but by faith. That's why the Bible clearly says, '*For if you confess with your mouth that Jesus is Lord and believe in your heart that God raised him from the dead, you will be saved. For it is by believing in your heart that you are made right with God, and it is by confessing with your mouth that you are saved.*'[13]

I knew that I had been totally forgiven. Every sin I had committed was washed away through the blood of Jesus Christ. Some of the things I did were so heinous I couldn't even write about them in this book. Things that would have condemned me to a lost eternity, sins that shouted loudly in my face 'Guilty' and would have made me endure the everlasting fire of hell. For hell is the abode of the damned, the place of everlasting conscious punishment in the fiery lake of burning sulphur.

Preachers have been accused of painting wrong pictures of hell and its fires of eternal torments. But they are only following the example of Christ, who graphically painted word pictures of hell to warn people of what would certainly come to all sinners who rejected the mercy of God. It never ceases to amaze me how people see the wrong in others and fail to see their own weaknesses. 'I'm a good sinner,' some have told me, fully believing that somehow they will escape the coming judgement.

There are two places for the dead to go – either heaven or hell. Heaven is a prepared place for prepared people. Forgiven sinners enter into the joy of heaven through the grace of God, brought to man by Jesus Christ's sacrificial death. Unforgiven sinners, who despise Jesus' mercy and offer of life, end up in hell, forever separated from God and in eternal torment.

The greatest words Jesus ever said to anyone were, '*My son, your sins are forgiven.*'[14] That's the incredible thing – a lifetime of wrongdoing can be put right in a moment. Some people find it hard to accept that God will give them a pardon from every sin they have ever committed. Once we receive Jesus Christ as our Saviour, God no longer deals with us as our sins deserve, but he forgives us freely and fully. In fact, King David, who had become an adulterer and murderer, after making confession to God, spoke about God's forgiveness in the Psalms: '*The Lord is merciful and gracious; he is slow to get angry and full of unfailing love. He will not constantly accuse us, nor remain angry forever. He has not punished us for all our sins, nor does he deal with us as we deserve. For his unfailing love toward those who fear him is as great as the height of the heavens above the earth. He has removed our rebellious acts as far away from us as the east is from the west.*'[15]

There was so much I had done wrong. Hundreds of people had been hurt by my callous crimes. Thousands of pounds worth of damage had been done to property; all those broken windows and jemmied doors that needed to be replaced. Broken-hearted people surveying their homes in the wake of my trail of burglary had felt violated and insecure in their own homes. Was it possible that I could be forgiven? God can forgive some, but what about people such as me, who are regarded as the scum of society. I was the sort of person they wanted to lock up and throw away the key. Could I be forgiven? Yes, with God there is forgiveness.

Later on, as I counselled a young man in the prison with another Christian inmate, he broke down, telling us that he had murdered his mum and could never be forgiven. What joy came to his face as we told him the greatest news ever: the blood of God's son, Jesus Christ, has power to cleanse us from all sin. In fact, there is no sin that, when repented of, cannot be dealt with by the blood of Jesus Christ.

Maybe, as you are reading this book right now, you are holding onto a dark secret, a burden, a sin committed and never confessed, and the weight of guilt is crushing your soul, robbing you of peace. Some sins are so depraved you would never think of speaking to a minister about them, lest he recoils from you in sheer horror. Yet, with God, there is mercy. His grace allows you the chance of repentance and the opportunity for you to come clean with him about your sins. Whatever you have done, know this – there is forgiveness with God; you can be made clean through the blood of Jesus. The world has many religions on offer for the spiritually hungry, but none of them offers hope for the guilty sinner awaiting judgement and hell fire, nor the peace and joy that comes with God's forgiveness.

At a great parliament of religions held in Chicago many years ago, practically every known religion was represented. During one session, Dr Joseph Cook of Boston, suddenly arose and said: 'Gentlemen, I beg to introduce to you a woman with a great sorrow.

Bloodstains are on her hands and nothing she has tried will remove them. The blood is that of murder. She has been driven to desperation in her distress. Is there anything in your religion that will remove her sin and give her peace?' A hush fell upon the gathering. Not one of the company replied. Raising his eyes heavenwards, Dr Cook then cried out, 'John, can you tell this woman how to get rid of her awful sin?' The great preacher waited, as if listening for a reply. Suddenly he cried, 'Listen, John speaks, "The blood of Jesus Christ, his Son, cleanses us from all sins." ' Not a soul broke the silence: the representatives of Eastern religions and Western cults sat dumb. In the face of human need, the Gospel of Jesus Christ alone could meet the need. The sin of the race demanded the blood of Christ.

From that moment in my cell on 19th December 1984, I knew a peace and a joy that I hadn't dreamed existed. Psalm 32 starts with, 'Oh, what joy for those whose rebellion is forgiven.' I had that joy deep within me, a joy that was different to all the euphoria that sex, drink and drugs had ever given me. God's joy is not dependent on external circumstances like the joyous feeling the world understands. Before this, my joy would rest upon the money in my back pocket, a girl on one arm and a bottle held in the other. If something threatened any of those factors, or removed them, then my feeling of happiness and joy quickly dissipated. The joy of Jesus is absolutely fantastic. I had years yet to serve at Aylesbury, long days to languish behind locked doors and barred windows. But now I really didn't care. I had found the answer to life; I

> *Oh, what joy for those whose rebellion is forgiven*

had discovered what it was that my heart had craved for over all those terrible years. Through that Gideon Bible left on the cell floor, I had made the greatest discovery of my life: one that had given me the greatest joy I had ever known.

The Greatest Discovery

Over the years, millions have discovered that Jesus Christ is the 'Pearl of great price', and when they give all that they have to own him, they possess the greatest treasure in the world.

In the year 1847, a doctor from Edinburgh, Sir James Simpson, discovered that chloroform could be used as an anaesthetic to render people insensible to the pain of surgery. From his early experiments, Dr Simpson made it possible for people to go through the most dangerous operations without fear of pain and suffering. Some people even claim that his was one of the most significant discoveries of modern medicine. Some years later, while lecturing at the University of Edinburgh, Dr Simpson was asked by one of his students, 'What do you consider to be the greatest discovery of your life-

My greatest discovery was when I discovered myself a sinner and that Jesus Christ was my Saviour

time?' To the surprise of his students, who had expected him to refer to chloroform, Dr Simpson replied, 'My greatest discovery was when I discovered myself a sinner and that Jesus Christ was my Saviour.'

I knew that God's presence was with me in my cell. An awesome sense of peace and holiness prevailed, mixed with a deep joy that seemed to bubble up and flow from

a well opened up within my heart. Wiping the tears from
my face, I grabbed the Bible and finding Matthew 6,
gazed at the words of Jesus as he taught the people what
we all know as 'The Lord's Prayer'. Using those words I
began to pray to God. I voiced my thoughts to God quietly and vocally. Afterwards, I poured out my heartfelt
thanks to my Heavenly Father, for now I realised that's
who he really is. I had made the greatest discovery any
man could make in finding Christ as Saviour. I didn't
realise the full extent of my discovery then, but I was later
to understand that my new life of faith in Jesus Christ had
made me seriously rich. As I climbed into my bed and
pulled the green prison blanket over me to keep out the
night chill, I knew that my life would never be the same
again.

9

SERIOUSLY RICH

The days following my salvation experience were ones of deep joy and wonderful peace. I was indeed a new person and the old things had passed away. My life of waste and ruin had been transformed – now I was seriously rich! The Bible says that *'The blessing of the Lord makes a person rich, and he adds no sorrow with it.'*[16]

And that was my experience. I had found in Jesus Christ true treasure that made me more than a millionaire; treasure that would satisfy my heart and give me a sense of inner joy that the biggest bank account could never buy. Jesus once told a parable about true treasure. *'The Kingdom of Heaven is like a treasure that a man discovered hidden in a field. In his excitement, he hid it again and sold everything he owned to get enough money to buy the field – and to get the treasure, too!'*[17]

I was like that man. I had stumbled over the treasure as I read the pages of the Bible. I realised that my lifestyle had made me poor, but the treasure Jesus Christ offered would make me seriously rich. I just had to own Christ, and so I was glad to sell all I had to possess him. I was only too pleased to give up my wrong lifestyle and perverted sense of values, to get my hands on the treasure of knowing God personally.

Daily, I continued to read my Bible, rejoicing at the treasures I discovered God had given me to make me rich through his son Jesus Christ. Yes, Jesus had brought me to a place of fabulous wealth, a wealth that has no limit, through his love and death for us on the cross. The Apostle Paul taught the church at Corinth this truth by saying, '*You know how full of love and kindness our Lord Jesus Christ was. Though he was very rich, yet for your sakes he became poor, so that by his poverty he could make you rich*'.[18]

> *Jesus had brought me to a place of fabulous wealth, a wealth that has no limit*

I knew I was seriously rich when I began to realise increasingly that I had a father in heaven who deeply loved me. I remember reading Isaiah 49 for the first time; a scripture that speaks about the possibility of a mother forgetting her child, but God saying that he would never forget his people. I was amazed when God spoke to me saying he had engraved my name upon the palms of his hands. That spoke to me of being unforgettable to God. People had forgotten Richard Pidgley, a criminal who had been lost in the prison system, now reduced to a mere number. My name, however, was ever before my father in heaven. I was unforgettable to him and, although I was locked away, I knew that God would remember my plight as he saw my name engraved upon his hands.

To have my name engraved on God's hands meant that my new relationship with God was invaluable to him. Engraving means to cut the image deep into the surface. If you pick up a trophy you can feel the engraving cut deep into the surface of the metal. My place in God's heart was of the utmost importance to him. This new relationship I had with him was no fleeting teenage love story, but something permanent, just as a name engraved into the surface of a trophy is permanent. That's why the Bible talks about adoption being part of the 'New Birth' experience. *'His unchanging plan has always been to adopt us into his own family by bringing us to himself through Jesus Christ. And this gave him great pleasure.'*[19]

Now, coming from my children's home background, I knew that fostering meant temporary care, and that although the care could be excellent, with all concerned being happy, there could, however, be no lasting security in the relationship. To be fostered meant that at any time you could be snatched away to a new home, whether you wanted it or not. In contrast, to be adopted was different. Once adopted into a family you had the full rights as a legitimate child of the family and the security that you belonged to the adopting parents, and that no cruel system could ever snatch you away from your home.

To be adopted by God was the most wonderful thing that had happened to me! I knew that I was totally secure in his hands and nothing would ever change that. I didn't have to worry that my new-found peace and happiness would be taken from me, because Jesus himself said, *'I give them eternal life, and they will never perish. No one will snatch them away from me, for my Father has given them to me, and he is more powerful than anyone else. So no one can take them from me. The Father and I are one.'*[20]

Billy Bray, the famous Cornish evangelist, who was a rough, hard drinking and sinful man before Christ marvellously saved him, recognised the great implications of his salvation. He, too, was seriously rich and so, when he discovered the wonder of 'adoption', went everywhere telling people with great joy, 'I'm the King's son!'

I knew that I was rich when I discovered the peace of God. For years I had not known much stability of either life or mind, but now I was filled with deep peace. My circumstances were far from peaceful, as the prison doors constantly banged shut on an ever-changing company of convicts, as men came and went. The Bible speaks of God as being our rock; a picture of strength and abiding security. That's what God had become to me now. When King David was relentlessly pursued by his enemies thousands of years ago, he found peace by trusting and abiding in God's presence. David described God as his rock and his fortress, in whom he could find rest and peace for his soul.

God's peace is supernatural and it kept me, in the midst of a very stressful situation. For many, the prison regime with its locked doors, claustrophobic cells and the unending threats of violence from prisoner to prisoner, is stressful. These things cause anxiety and that was something I had suffered from for many years. But now, the outward circumstances no longer troubled me, as, deep inside, God's peace kept my heart and soul in perfect rest.

Yes, I was seriously rich because I was forgiven, I had been set free. I now had a new and meaningful friendship with God; I was no longer alone but part of the great family of God that has members in every nation of the world; I was enjoying fullness of life just as Jesus had promised and I had a future that was totally secure, a future so bright that it burnt my eyes!

My time in Aylesbury eventually came to an end, but not before I had had some great adventures in God behind the bars! I learnt to share my 'Treasure' with others and saw first-hand the mighty power of God saving, healing and delivering other captives. Before my very eyes I saw the wonderful and powerful transformation of men who had been sentenced to life for murder, with no hope of early release, finding new life in Jesus.

I was released in 1985 and went to Gloucester where I was offered a place at Victory Outreach, a Christian ministry helping young people who had been through the prison system. I lived at Victory Outreach for about a year, and in that time visited many prisons sharing my story with hundreds of men. At weekends I attended Robinswood Pentecostal Church, and it was there that I met the girl of my dreams!

Lynne was a young woman who attended Robinswood Pentecostal Church and who had given up her job to come to Victory Outreach to serve God. From the time of our first meeting I knew she was the one for me! She was a great girl, intelligent, attractive, fun-loving, hard-working but, even more important, a girl who loved Jesus just as much as I did. God spoke to my heart and told me to ask her to marry me! Knowing that God never makes mistakes, I waited for the right moment. One day I managed to get her to come with me to visit a man in Featherstone Prison. Waiting to go into the prison, Lynne and I sat outside the gates in the warm sunshine of a summer's day. The moment was not romantic by any means – but right. So I got down on one knee and asked Lynne to marry me. And of course she said, 'Yes'. So, on the 19 September 1987, we were married at Robinswood Pentecostal Church, Gloucester. We made a decision to put God first in our lives, and because of that we have enjoyed God's richest blessings over many years.

Two of the greatest blessings we have received from God since we have been married are our two sons, Josh and Sam. Those two boys have been the joy and rejoicing of our hearts; they have given us sleepless nights and some grey hairs too! Raising my two sons has taught me so much about our relationship with God. Watching them relating to me and asking me for help with such simple trust, has brought me to a greater place of trust in my Heavenly Father. Through the simple lessons of parenting I have come to a greater understanding of what it really means to be a child of God. I guess that nothing really prepares you for parenthood, and along the way I have certainly made some mistakes but, thankfully, God has continuously helped me in my role of being a dad. Both Josh and Sam, now young men, have a personal faith in Christ. They are also musically gifted and it's a real joy to see them both actively serving God in praise and worship ministry. As I watch Josh and Sam becoming young adults, I can't stop thanking God for blessing me with two great sons and, yes, I am really proud of them.

In the early 1990s, God clearly told Lynne and me that it was time to start our public ministry, so I trained as an Assemblies of God minister and was ordained in April 1996. Since those early days of ministry Lynne and I have had many exciting adventures serving God together, including leading several churches and ministering in many other places throughout the UK. We are currently enjoying an itinerant ministry preaching and teaching the Word of God and also focusing on encouraging and supporting church leaders. Over the years we have met many wonderful people and visited some great places. Our ministry to date has taken us to Ireland, France, South Africa, Australia, Malaysia, Poland, Java, Borneo, India, Egypt, Albania, The Philippines, Spain and the United States of America. It's been our great joy to

> *Lynne and I have had many exciting adventures serving God together*

have been able to share the gospel in these nations and an even greater joy to have seen countless lives which were ruined, just like mine, gloriously transformed through the power of Jesus Christ.

10

YOU TOO CAN BE SERIOUSLY RICH

Some time ago, I was invited to speak at a church in Gloucester. I was preaching on how Jesus Christ had changed my life, making me seriously rich: not in bank notes and gold, but in true riches, such as God's love, joy and peace. As I was bringing my message to a conclusion, a man stood to his feet and began to walk down the aisle toward the pulpit where I was standing. With tears in his eyes, and with a loud voice he kept saying, 'I want what Richard's got!'

I fought back tears myself, as the pastor came forward and put his loving arms around this man and quietly led him to Jesus Christ, through a simple prayer of repentance and faith.

Maybe as you have read this book there is a voice calling out from the emptiness of your heart saying, 'I want what Richard's got.' The good news is that you can possess what I have, for you, too, can know Jesus Christ as your personal Saviour. That's why I quoted the words of the song at the beginning of the book . . .

It is no secret what God can do.
What he's done for others, he'll do for you!

No one is beyond God's love. The Bible clearly says, '*For God so loved the world . . .* ' meaning that if you're reading this book, on this beautiful planet we call 'earth', then God's love is extended to you. God wants to make you seriously rich. He wants to fill your whole life with true treasure that will satisfy your heart and make you the happiest person on earth.

There is no magic formula to becoming the person God longs for you to be. There is no ritualistic service to make you the brand new person for whom Jesus died. At the front of Robinswood Pentecostal Church (now known as 'One Church') there used to be some thought-provoking words stuck on to the plain brick wall in large clear letters **'ONLY BELIEVE'**. The Gospel is simple so that every one of us can grasp it and enjoy its marvellous truth. Over the weeks and years, I have seen countless people turn their lives over to Jesus Christ: from

> *Jesus is not intimidated by how bad your past is, as his power can remove your guilt and bring you into a marvellous future*

those who have all that the world offers, to those who literally have nothing. They come to a life-changing faith in Christ. I have heard many stories just like mine, and many far worse. Jesus is not intimidated by how bad your past is, as his power can remove your guilt and bring you into a marvellous future.

Jesus Christ is the mighty Son of God who can transform your life into something beautiful, just as he did mine. He is all powerful and if you come to him with simple faith, trusting in his word as I did, he will turn your . . . Guilty to Not Guilty . . . Death to Life . . . Darkness to Light . . . Hatred to Love . . . Weakness to Power . . . Bondage to Freedom . . . Tribulation to

Triumph . . . Grief to Joy . . . Gloom to Glory . . . Defeat to Victory . . . Failure to Success . . . Fear to Faith . . . I Can't to I Can!

Yes, when you believe in Jesus Christ and come to him, not only can he make you seriously rich, he also will seriously change your whole life. That's why Jesus talked about being 'born again'. He literally gives you the incredible experience of starting a completely new life.

We often sing a little song in our church that helps express the wonderful change that Jesus has brought to those who have come to him by faith . . .

> *Something beautiful, something good,*
> *All my confusion he understood.*
> *All I had to offer him, was brokenness and strife,*
> *But he made something beautiful of my life.*[21]

If you truly want to be seriously rich, by enjoying the abundant, exciting life that only Jesus Christ can offer, you need to do two vital things. First, you must repent. That means turning away from the things you are doing wrong and turn to God. Jesus was absolutely clear about repentance: '*"At last the time has come!" he announced. "The Kingdom of God is near! Turn from your sins and believe this Good News!"*'[22]

Jesus was telling the people to repent, to acknowledge their sins, to change their minds and the whole way they lived their lives. We have been running away from God, living life our own way, but repentance means we stop running away from God and do a U-turn so that, in fact, we are now running to God.

Many people get confused over the issue of sin. Because they have never committed crimes such as I had done, they feel they are righteous and probably should have no problem with an entrance one day into heaven. Sin is more than somebody breaking the law of the land: it's man's choice to reject God and defiantly stand in rebellion against him and all he desires for our lives. People everywhere are breaking the Ten Commandments all the time! God's moral codes for happy and holy living are flouted and trodden underfoot by the masses who consider that they are right with God because of their own DIY set of moral codes and occasional church attendance. In fact, the attitude of self-righteousness is far more deadly than sins committed openly. That's why the Bible says, *'The human heart is most deceitful and desperately wicked.'* [23]

Self-righteousness is certainly deceiving many people. God sees and knows the thoughts, intents and actions of every heart and says, *'For all have sinned; all fall short of God's glorious standard.'* [24]

There is no getting away from the truth, as painful as it seems to many 'good' people. We must accept the fact that we are all sinful because of free choice. Every one of us, no matter how rich or famous, needs a Saviour to remove our sins and replace them with his righteousness to make us acceptable to the God who created the universe. Gerrit Gustafson, a modern hymn-writer, put it like this,

Only by grace can we enter, only by grace can we stand;
Not by our human endeavour, but by the blood of the lamb
Into your presence you call us, call us to come.
Into your presence you draw us and now by your grace we come.

Lord, if you mark our transgression, who would stand?

Lord, if you mark our transgressions, who would stand?
Thanks to your grace we are cleansed by the blood of the Lamb.[25]

Unlike many who resist the convicting presence of God's Holy Spirit, I was in no doubt that I was a sinner and needed to be saved. Repentance means that we must also confess our sins to God. To confess our sins is more than just admitting them and saying a quick 'sorry', like a child wanting to appease an angry parent. Confession actually means to see our sins through the eyes of God: in other words, to feel the way God does about all we do wrong. Now, that is more than a quick 'sorry'. I saw that my sins were so defiling and depraved that they had angered God and caused him to place the death sentence upon me, eternal hell.

When I saw the Cross as God's greatest demonstration of love ever manifested in all eternity, I loathed my sins that placed Christ through such agony. I hated my sins, which brought Jesus to this world, to be despised and rejected, to be arrested, to be mocked, to be whipped until the flesh hung off his back. To have a crown of cruel thorns thrust upon his brow and then to be made to carry his own cross through the maddened crowd; the blood from his wounds dripping along the way, leaving a trail to be callously trampled underfoot by shouting, abusive people who followed to see the final spectacle as a naked man was nailed to a cross and lifted up to die in excruciating pain.

The second vital thing we must do is to believe in and receive, Jesus Christ as our Saviour. To do that, we must ask him into our hearts to take up residence: to sit upon the throne of our lives, to be our Lord and to make the changes that are needed deep within us. I used to work with an evangelist in Northern Ireland who regularly spoke to large crowds about God's amazing grace and the life changing power of Jesus Christ. Every time he finished his message, he closed with this challenge, 'There is a God in heaven who loves you. He sent his Son to die for you and he can change your life – but you have to let him!' Will you let God change your life? Why not make the following prayer your prayer, and be amazed at what God will do for you.

Father God

Thank you for sending Jesus to let me know just how much you love and care for me and how you want to be first in my life.

Father I am sorry for living my life without you – I am really sorry for my sin, my selfishness and at times my shameful behaviour, please forgive me.

Thank you for allowing Jesus to die in my place on the cross so that I can be restored back to you. I now believe that through Jesus I can be totally forgiven and receive the gift of eternal life. Lord Jesus please come into my life right now and be my Lord and Saviour.

Amen

God promises to hear all those who call to him through the name of his Son Jesus Christ. If you sincerely prayed that prayer and really meant it, then you are now saved, and seriously rich. As the Bible says, *'For if you confess with your mouth that Jesus is Lord and believe in your heart that God raised him from the dead, you will be saved.'*[26]

What will you do next?

This book is now almost finished, and it's time for me to lay down my pen. In closing, however, I can't help wondering to myself, what will you do next? If you have read about what Jesus Christ has done for me and have a little faith because of my story, then you are like the man who walked through the field and found treasure. You see, Jesus Christ is the greatest discovery that anyone can ever make. The question is, what will you do with the discovery? Will you walk away and forget about it? To do so, would mean that you have passed up the world's greatest treasure: riches that will certainly bless your life beyond your wildest dreams. Or, will you be like the man that Jesus spoke of, who sold everything he had so that he could go and buy the field and possess the discovered treasure?[27]

I will have to leave that decision with you. As for me, I am going to continue to enjoy my discovery of new life in Jesus Christ – treasure indeed that has made me seriously rich.

WHAT NEXT?

Maybe you have read my story and decided to trust Jesus Christ as your Saviour. If you prayed the simple prayer that I included in Chapter 10, you will have asked Jesus Christ into your life. Congratulations, you are now saved! Now that you are 'born again' through the power of God, all things will become new, life will never be the same again, your poverty has been turned to God's prosperity. In fact, you are seriously rich because . . .

1. Jesus Christ Has Come Into Your Life

It's incredible, God, who created the vastness and splendour of the universe, can live anywhere he wants to – and he chose your heart! Because you have invited God into your life to take up residence and to reign in your heart, he will prove to you day by day his great faithfulness. God says . . . *'I will never fail you. I will never forsake you.'*[28]

2. You Have Been Completely Forgiven

That's right! Everything you have ever done wrong is forgiven and forgotten by God. The Bible says . . . *'He cancelled the record that contained the charges against us. He took it and destroyed it by nailing it to Christ's cross.'*[29]

3. You Will Start To Experience 'Life' As God Intended

Up to now, you have been separated from God because of your sins. Sin separates us from God and separation from God means it's impossible to enjoy life to the full. As my friend once said . . . 'You can have a full life, but without Jesus, it's not life to the full!' Jesus said . . . *'My purpose is to give life in all its fullness!'*[30]

Not long after becoming a Christian I started singing a little song that summed up my wonderful life-changing experience in Jesus Christ:

> *Jesus makes the difference in me*
> *Jesus makes the difference in me*
> *Once my heart was bound by sin*
> *But now praise God it's free*
> *For Jesus makes the difference in me!*[31]

If you have accepted Jesus Christ as your Lord and Saviour you can be absolutely sure that you now have new life because the Bible says . . . *'And this is what God has testified: he has given us eternal life, and this life is in his Son. So whoever has God's Son has life; whoever does not have his Son does not have life. I write this to you who believe in the Son of God, so that you may know you have eternal life.'*[32]

When you experience new life in Jesus it's like being 'born again'. You are now like a 'baby' spiritually – but don't worry, God wants you to grow! God has provided you with the means for strong, healthy Christian growth, so that you can live for his glory and know what it is to be victorious over the power of sin.

Steps For Christian Growth

Get to know God by reading the Bible every day.

The Bible says . . . *'All Scripture is inspired by God and is useful to teach us what is true and to make us realize what is wrong in our lives. It straightens us out and teaches us to do what is right. It is God's way of preparing us in every way, fully equipped for every good thing God wants us to do.'*[33]

Relate to God by praying to him every day.

The Bible says . . . *'Don't worry about anything; instead, pray about everything. Tell God what you need, and thank him for all he has done.'*[34]

Obey God in the things you know you should every day.

The Bible says . . . *'And now, just as you accepted Christ Jesus as your Lord, you must continue to live in obedience to him.'*[35]

Walk in the power of God's Holy Spirit every day.

The Bible says . . . *'When I think of the wisdom and scope of God's plan, I fall to my knees and pray to the Father, the Creator of everything in heaven and on earth. I pray that from his glorious, unlimited resources he will give you mighty inner strength through his Holy Spirit.'*[36]

Tell other people about what Jesus has done for you as much as you can.

Jesus said . . . *'If anyone acknowledges me publicly here on earth, I will openly acknowledge that person before my Father in heaven.'*[37]

Have fellowship with other Christians by attending a good evangelical church.

The Bible says . . . *'And all the believers met together constantly and shared everything they had. They sold their possessions and shared the proceeds with those in need. They worshiped together at the Temple each day, met in homes for the Lord's Supper, and shared their meals with great joy and generosity.'*[38]

The Bible says . . . *'And let us not neglect our meeting together, as some people do, but encourage and warn each other, especially now that the day of his coming back again is drawing near.'*[39]

If you would like to talk to someone about the Bible and its message of life through Jesus Christ, why not contact your local branch of The Gideons. You can find their local contact number in the telephone directory under 'The Gideons International'.

Richard Pidgley can be contacted through AOG UK.

REFERENCES

1. 2 Corinthians 8:9. Scripture taken from the THE MESSAGE. Copyright © by Eugene H. Peterson, 1993, 1994, 1995, 1996, 2000, 2001, 2002. Used by permission of NavPress Publishing Group.
2. 'It is No Secret' by Stuart Hamblen © 1950 Hamblen Music Co., California.
3. 2 Corinthians 5:17
4. Jo Izatt
5. Jeremiah 17:9
6. Ephesians 3:20
7. John 3:16
8. John 15:13 KING JAMES VERSION.
9. 1 John 1:5–9
10. Matthew 6:5–7. Scripture taken from the THE MESSAGE. Copyright © 1993,1994, 1995, 1996, 2000, 2001, 2002. Used by permission of NavPress Publishing Group.
11. Revelation 20:11–15
12. Revelation 3:20
13. Romans 10:9–10
14. Mark 2:5
15. Psalm 103:8–12
16. Proverbs 10:22
17. Matthew 13:44

18. 2 Corinthians 8:9
19. Ephesians 1:5
20. John 10:28–30
21. 'Something Beautiful' by William and Gloria Gaither © 1971 William J. Gaither.
22. Mark 1:15
23. Jeremiah 17:9.
24. Romans 3:23
25. 'Only by Grace' by Gerrit Gustafson Copyright © 1990 Integrity's Hosanna! Music. Adm. Kingsway's Thankyou Music.
26. Romans 10:9
27. Matthew 13:44
28. Hebrews 13:5
29. Colossians 2:14
30. John 10:10
31. 'Jesus Makes the Difference in Me' source unknown.
32. 1 John 5:11–13
33. 2 Timothy 3:16–17
34. Philippians 4:6
35. Colossians 2:6
36. Ephesians 3:14–16
37. Matthew 10:32
38. Acts 2:44–46
39. Hebrews 10:25

Logos Ministries International

LMI is an interdenominational Christian organisation founded in 1977 by Thomas and Yvonne McClean. It is involved in four key areas of work: a Mission Awareness Programme, Bible Teaching Ministry, Overseas Ministry Programme and Youth & Schools Outreach.

Through the **Mission Awareness Programme** LMI aims to inspire and challenge individuals and churches to get involved in mission. Christians around the world are being trained to be effective disciples and leaders are being equipped through LMI's **Bible Teaching Ministry.** The **Overseas Ministry Programme** is committed to working in partnership with the national church to help fulfil the Great Commission by assisting its spiritual development and funding specific projects. The **Youth & Schools Outreach** seeks to bring the claims and challenges of Christ to today's young people in a relevant way. LMI has distributed thousands of copies of *Seriously Rich* to secondary school students to help them explore the Christian faith.

If you would like to find out more about LMI go to: www.lmi-org.net

Logos Ministries International
7–8 Bellsbridge Office Park
Ladas Drive
Belfast
BT6 9FH
Northern Ireland

Telephone: +44 02890458362
Email: info@lmi-org.net

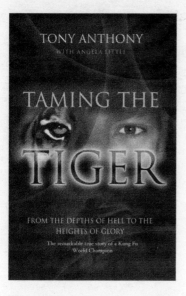

Taming the Tiger

From the Depths of Hell to the Heights of Glory The Remarkable True Story of a Kung Fu World Champion

Tony Anthony with Angela Little

Tony Anthony knew no fear. Three-times World Kung Fu Champion, he was self-assured, powerful and at the pinnacle of his art. An extraordinary career awaited him.

This fast-paced, compelling and, at times, chilling account is Tony's deeply moving true story. More extraordinary than fantasy, more remarkable than fiction, this blockbusting read almost defies belief. With fascinating insight into China's martial arts, and the knife-edge adrenaline highs of the bodyguard lifestyle, it documents the personal tragedy that turned a 'disciple of enlightenment' into a bloodthirsty, violent man.

From the depths of hell in Cyprus's notorious Nicosia Central Prison, all might have been lost, but for the visits of a stranger . . .

978-1-86024-481-0

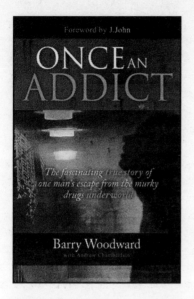

Once an Addict

The Fascinating True Story of One Man's Escape from the Murky Drugs Underworld

Barry Woodward
with Andrew Chamberlain

Barry Woodward was a drug dealer and heroin addict who once lived on the notorious Bull Rings in the centre of Manchester. *Once an Addict* describes Barry's descent into the murky underworld of drug dealing, addiction, crime and imprisonment. Along the way we are introduced to some of the most extraordinary characters, and we see the extreme lengths to which some of them will go to get their next 'fix'. Illegal drug use claimed the lives of many such people, and it seemed inevitable that Barry would also succumb to the consequences of his addiction.

With devastating amphetamine-induced mental health issues, a fourteen-year heroin addiction, a string of broken relationships, and the threat of HIV looming, the outlook for Barry appeared very bleak. Then three extraordinary encounters changed his life forever . . .

978-1-86024-602-9

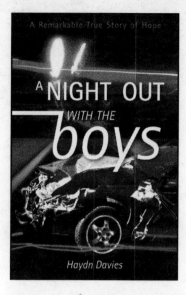

A Night Out with the Boys

A Remarkable True Story of Hope

Haydn Davies

Haydn was an ordinary lad with an extraordinary gift. Selected for the Welsh under-21 football team at a young age, he had a promising career ahead. Yet all of this disappeared after a sudden car accident. He was propelled into a life of uncertainty, his spinal cord almost severed. Faced with a future of operations and wheelchairs, things looked bleak. But why? Why had this happened? Was it for a reason?

978-1-85078-735-8

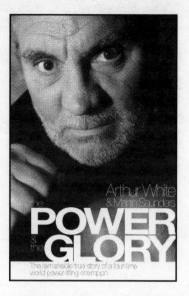

The Power &
the Glory

*The Remarkable Story of
a Four-Time World
Powerlifting Champion*

*Arthur White &
Martin Saunders*

Arthur White had it all. Not only was he a successful businessman and happy family man, but as a champion powerlifter, he was literally on top of the world. But when he got to the top, he wasn't satisfied . . .

As he searched for a greater high, Arthur's life spiralled out of control. Drug addiction, an intense affair and a descent into violence followed, and before long death seemed like the only way out. As he stared into the abyss, an incredible encounter turned Arthur's life upside down. He would never be the same again . . .

978-1-86024-560-2